Praise for Alex Partridge and *Now It All Makes Sense*

'This book shows ADHD isn't just for little boys – it's for everyone. From relationships to entrepreneurs, finance to parenting, this provides validation, hope and clarity for all of us who have felt both "too much" and "not enough" as we are. A must-read to connect the dots of ADHD in yourself and others.'

Leanne Maskell, founder of ADHD Works and author of *ADHD: An A to Z*

'I've learnt so much from Alex and sighed with so many "Aha" moments that I haven't seen in books before. Thank you for making us feel seen, heard and celebrated!'

Martine McCutcheon

'Alex is rich, successful and an entertaining and concise communicator. Alex is also very ADHD. You want to read this book for all these reasons. It helps that it is short.'

Kate Spicer, author, journalist and documentary maker

'Truly life changing. The perfect antidote for shame.'

Samantha Hiew PhD, founder of ADHD Girls

'A powerhouse of a book. Deeply validating.'

Rich and Roxanne Pink (ADHD Love)

'This book's ability to present an alternative perspective on ADHD, where individuals develop a profound understanding of their neurodiverse brain and recognise its unique advantages, is incredible. Rather than seeing ADHD as something that holds an individual back, it highlights how it can elevate one's capacity to contribute to society. This is a much-needed book in today's world.'

TJ Power, neuroscientist

'Alex's honest and open story is a gift to people who have ADHD and their family and friends. It's a story full of hope and inspiration, as Alex shares his personal experience of living and thriving with ADHD.'

Dr Mark Rackley, psychologist

Now It All
Makes Sense

How an ADHD Diagnosis Brought
Clarity to My Life

Alex Partridge

sheldon **PRESS**

First published in Great Britain by Sheldon Press in 2025
An imprint of John Murray Press

15

This book is for information or educational purposes only and is not intended to act as a
substitute for medical advice or treatment. Any person with a condition requiring medical
attention should consult a qualified medical practitioner or suitable therapist.

A CIP catalogue record for this title is available from the British Library

Trade Paperback ISBN 978 1 399 81781 3
ebook ISBN 978 1 399 81782 0

Typeset by KnowledgeWorks Global Ltd.

Printed and bound in Great Britain by Clays Ltd, Elcograf S.p.A.

John Murray Press policy is to use papers that are natural, renewable and recyclable
products and made from wood grown in sustainable forests. The logging and
manufacturing processes are expected to conform to the environmental regulations of the
country of origin.

John Murray Press
Carmelite House
50 Victoria Embankment
London EC4Y 0DZ

www.sheldonpress.co.uk

John Murray Press, part of Hodder & Stoughton Limited
An Hachette UK company

The authorised representative in the EEA is Hachette Ireland, 8 Castlecourt
Centre, Dublin 15, D15 XTP3, Ireland (email: info@hbgi.ie)

Dedicated to all the late diagnosed ADHDers.
You were always enough.

Table of Contents

Introduction   ix

1 Feeling different   1

2 Finding our ADHD strengths
   (and working out how to use them)   23

3 Money can't buy a new neurotype
   (how to manage our addictions)   49

4 Making friends with our worst enemy: rejection   71

5 Our love languages   95

6 Dodging the ADHD tax   117

7 Preparing myself for parenting   137

8 How to start a business when you have ADHD   159

9 Romance that works with your ADHD,
   not against it   193

10 Advice for my younger self   215

Endnotes   239

Acknowledgements   241

Index   242

Introduction

I was 34 years old when a psychiatrist looked me in the eyes and said my attention deficit hyperactivity disorder (ADHD) was 'clear as hell'.

I won't forget the shock. It was a diagnosis I thought I would never receive. After all, I was never physically hyperactive. I was taught that ADHD was what naughty little boys have. Boys who throw stones at windows and topple classroom tables over. That wasn't me. I was always very still. Physically still, at least.

My mind was always very active. I enjoyed being creative and finding solutions to problems. When I was six years old, I remember being hyper-fixated on designing a board game. I rummaged through my parents' cupboards, found all the board games, located the manufacturer details on the box and sent my board game design to them all.

Weeks went past with no response. Then one day, my mum told me there was a letter for me. It read, 'Dear Alex, Thank you for your design. Unfortunately, we're not looking for new game designs at present. However, we greatly admire your entrepreneurial spirit. Always lean into that. Kindest regards, Board Game Company.'

So, I did exactly that. I leant into my entrepreneurial spirit (well, after I asked my mum what the word 'entrepreneurial' meant). On the weekends, I washed cars. After school, I sold apples outside the house. I tried anything and everything to keep my racing mind occupied. Even if my interest in that 'thing' didn't always last more than a few weeks!

The problems came when I was at school. Being forced to sit in a classroom and focus on something I wasn't interested in. Being acutely tuned into my surroundings, noticing patterns in people's behaviours and therefore feeling paranoid about everyone's opinion of me. There was no way for me to vent my racing mind, no way for me to release the pressure.

One day, the teacher pointed at me and said, 'Alex, do you know the answer to this question?' In that moment, all the other children turned to look at me. I felt my face going red. I could feel my palms going sweaty and my heart rate increasing. I stood up abruptly and marched out of the classroom.

I found someone in the corridor and said, 'Please call an ambulance. I'm having a heart attack.' I wasn't having a heart attack, I was having an anxiety attack. This was the first time I had heard the word 'anxiety'.

It was horrible and it made me scared of classrooms. It made me scared of school. I refused to go back and after several games of dad chasing me around the garden desperately trying to get me in the car, my parents moved me to another school.

But the problem persisted. At 15 years old I was diagnosed with generalized anxiety disorder and put on beta blockers and antidepressants. They didn't help. I stopped taking them after six weeks. If I'm honest with you, they made me feel worse.

At 18 years old I discovered alcohol and quickly figured out it turned down the volume in my head. It also nearly killed me, but I'll speak more about that later. Often being a pleasure-seeking individual with low impulse control, it wasn't a shock when I discovered the strong link between ADHD and addiction.

I've spoken to 50 ADHD experts on my podcast, *ADHD Chatter*. Psychiatrists, psychologists, doctors, behavioural experts, ADHD accountants, ADHD lawyers, ADHD nutritionists, addiction specialists, ADHD coaches, ADHD CEOs, ADHD parents, ADHD police officers, ADHD marriage counsellors and many people with ADHD lived experiences. With every conversation, it became more obvious that ADHD was present throughout my life.

When someone told me that ADHD hyperactivity can be internalized, my whole life made sense. It gave me the hyper-focus that enabled me to create two global social media brands, but when not channelled into a task I enjoyed it has been the cause of great anxiety.

I've always been entrepreneurial, but I had poor financial skills and often lost interest in projects before I finished them. I own an impressive list of domains.

I enjoy buying things, but it often results in overspending and financial difficulties.

I love meeting new people, but I've always struggled to maintain friendships.

I've always fallen in love deeply, but my sensitivity to rejection has made it hard to sustain relationships.

If I had been born with the understanding of ADHD I have now, my life would have been very different. So much pain would have been avoided.

I wish I could go back in time with the knowledge I have accumulated, put my arms around the younger version of me, the little boy having that anxiety attack in the school corridor, and tell him, you're not broken. You don't need to be fixed. Your brain works a little bit differently. And with the right tools, you can mitigate the challenges and lean into the strengths and ultimately achieve amazing things.

I wish I could tell him, 'Everything is going to be OK.'

I wish I could tell him there's a solution.

I wish I could give him this book.

1

Feeling different

One of my early school memories is from when I was four or five years old. The other kids had gone to play outside, but I had somehow hidden under the teacher's desk. I waited silently in the dark until the class slowly filled back up with noisy children, got out from my hiding spot and sat back in my seat. The teacher never noticed I was missing.

As I got older, similar instances of isolating myself continued. Instead of playing with other children at break time, I would spend those 30 minutes in the library, flicking through the comic books. Sometimes I would lock myself in the toilet until I heard the bell ring.

For as long as I can remember, I've had a suspicion that I am unusual.

Pretending to be something I wasn't

As a child, when I did interact with people, I found myself copying their mannerisms and their tone of voice.

I even pretended to share their interests and hobbies. I altered who I was in order to appear likeable to whoever I was with.

The most common example of this was when someone asked me what football team I supported. I never liked football, but I always said 'Manchester United'. Or when someone asked me if I knew of, or liked, a particular band or a film, I always said 'yes'. I then dreaded them asking a follow-up question because it would reveal my ignorance and make me go red in the face.

I never felt comfortable in my own skin. After I finished watching a film, I would act like the main character for days or even weeks, until I got bored and moved on to something else.

There was also a deep fear of confrontation, which meant I often said 'yes' to things I didn't want to do. On one occasion, I was asked if I wanted to sleep over at another boy's house. The initial idea sounded fun – we both liked the same computer game. However, every morning, his mother asked me if I wanted to stay another night. I didn't. I was desperate to get back home. But of course I said 'yes' – and ended up staying nearly a week until she said I couldn't stay any longer.

I got into so many situations like that. An initial excitement for something would make me impulsively say 'yes!', but then I would be trapped in that situation as I didn't know how to have the conversation required for me to leave.

It caused me plenty of problems when I started employment – but more on that later.

My suspicion that I was unusual, different, was confirmed soon after I started secondary school when a classmate said to me, 'Alex, you could be one of the cool kids if you weren't so weird. Why can't you just be *normal*?'

When I walked around school, it was with a conscious effort to maintain good posture. My natural walking style would have been looking at my feet and getting to my destination as fast as possible. However, I had once heard someone say a confident person walked slowly, with their head held high. But no one was fooled. When I was 16 years old, one of my teachers jokingly announced to the class, 'Alex pretends to be more confident than he is.'

He saw straight through me.

The difference I felt ran deep. For example, I've always felt that I experience emotions more profoundly than everyone else, even if I don't always show them. They overwhelm me and I don't always know where they come from. Throughout my childhood, if something exciting was announced – I was getting a new pair of shoes, or my favourite film was about to start – I would be simply overwhelmed with joy. And these emotions seemingly come out of nowhere – suddenly I'll be hyper-focused on a particular memory and burst into tears, or I'll find myself fixating on a particular injustice and feel angry.

My justice sensitivity flare-ups

I was only five years old when I felt my first justice sensitivity flare-up.

During playtime at school, I noticed some of the other children were digging holes in the dry mud. They were using their bare hands to pick away bits of mud, which made the process mind-numbingly slow. At home, my parents were having some renovation work done. I sneaked into a bedroom that was being redecorated and found a small bag of nails. 'Amazing!' I thought. 'They'll make a perfect digging tool.' I took the nails into school, feeling a huge amount of accomplishment as I handed them to the other children. I'd solved a problem, found them a solution.

Later the same day, one of the children cut his hand on one of the nails. 'Where did these nails come from?' asked the teacher. Immediately, I confessed. 'What a stupid thing to do!' the teacher yelled at me. My parents were called in and we all had a meeting to talk about how dangerous the nails were.

I remember sitting silently in that meeting, raging at the situation. I never intended to hurt anyone and yet I was being treated as if I had. My five-year-old mind simply thought the nails were a clever solution to a problem, but I was being called stupid.

Looking back now, obviously I can see it was an irresponsible thing to do. I could have *really* hurt someone. But at the time, the reaction from the teacher clashed directly with what I believed internally to be true and a silent, but painful, explosion took place inside me. It felt horrible.

I don't clean because my room is a mess. I clean because my mind is a mess. When I was younger – and still today – I found the solution to this horrible feeling often lay in cleaning.

After the nail incident at school, I calmed my mind by picking up all the loose leaves in the playground. When I got home, I tidied my room.

I always found the process of cleaning very soothing. Of course, when I was at my happiest, my bedroom was at its messiest! When I was just seven years old and my parents told me my pet hamster had passed away while I was at school, the sadness was unbearable. What did I do? I rushed upstairs to my bedroom and began cleaning.

My pet peeve was (still is) when someone else cleaned my room. It looked chaotic to the outside eye, but I knew where everything was. I knew my PlayStation controller was under my bed, in the left corner, right behind the old shoebox.

The cleaning was totally unpredictable, too. I could be in bed, about to fall asleep, and I'd suddenly leap out of bed and begin to clean my entire room.

I'm now 35 years old and I still only clean when I'm feeling stressed (or if I know someone is coming over in the next 30 minutes). Add some music into the situation and it's pure bliss.

Eye contact is weird

Another thing that made me feel different: I've always struggled with the concept of 'eye contact'.

Before my diagnosis, when people were talking to me, all I could hear was my internal monologue saying, 'Make sure you maintain eye contact, so they know you're listening.' This always prevented me from actually listening.

And I never knew which eye to look at because you can't look at both. *Should I look at the left eye? That seems intense. Okay, let's switch between the two, which also looks weird. I know, let's look at their nose.* Bingo!

Because of all that internal chatter, there's a zero per cent chance I'd actually hear, let alone remember, anything you said. It's why I constantly missed social cues – because I literally didn't hear them. Instead, I would smile and say 'that's good', oblivious to the fact that they had just informed me their cherished pet had died.

I found it much easier to focus on what the person was saying when I was looking away. This worked well most of the time, until looking away resulted in me seeing something that got my attention. Then I would instantly forget that someone was talking to me.

It looked like I was zoning out, but I was actually zoning *in* on something else. It's resulted in so much conflict over the years. For example, if I'm sitting in a restaurant with someone, I find it hard to pay attention because there's so much noise around me. I pick up on bits of other conversations. I'm making assumptions in my head about which tables are hosting a first date and which tables are hosting a long-married couple. This mental process is often interrupted by the person I'm with saying, 'Alex, did you even hear what I just said?'

As I got older I realized it was considered rude not to maintain good eye contact, so I forced myself to do it. As a result, I rarely remembered most conversations, which would make me feel anxious about bumping into that person again because I knew I didn't remember their name.

You could have either my eye contact or my undivided attention. But you couldn't have both.

Sometimes, now, when I'm struggling, I stare directly at the speaker's mouth. It helps me hear the words. Because of this, and for many other reasons, social interactions always caused me a lot of anxiety, which also got in the way of me remembering what was spoken about.

A striking example of this behaviour still happens whenever I walk my dog. If you're a dog owner, you'll know how regularly you bump into the same people in the park. We get into small talk, exchange names, speculate on the ages of each other's dogs, comment on how nice/bad the weather is and walk on. However, as I walk away, all I can think about is whether or not I sounded silly in that social encounter. They didn't like me. In fact, they hated me and this will be confirmed when I bump into them next time and have to ask, again, how old their dog is. The thought is unbearably awkward. I need to find a new park, I can't possibly go back to this one.

The sixth sense that nobody else had

One thing that made me feel the most different from others was heightened intuition. I have always been able to 'read' people exceptionally well. I can tell when someone's not being genuine. I'm a human lie detector.

I've got such early memories of watching politicians on TV and thinking, 'I don't trust that person.' So I've always felt a little smug when someone in the public eye gets ousted as a wrong 'un and I can say, 'See! I told you there was something off about them.'

Did you know that only 7 per cent of communication is verbal[1] – the actual words that come out of people's mouths? I don't know about you, but I've always been able to feel the other 93 per cent as well. I hear the tiny fluctuations in their tone of voice. I see the micro changes in their facial expression that reveal their true intentions. I'm hyper-aware of everything and everyone around me.

As I got older and entered the business world, I would pick up on everything in the office. I'd notice tiny fluctuations in room temperature. I'd wonder why that person slammed the door harder than normal. Why were their footsteps heavier today? Did they just give the boss an *eye roll*?

I knew that David from the accounts department was having an affair with Susan from HR. I could see their tiny, subconscious bodily flirtations that they didn't even know they were doing.

In the past, I used to interrupt people a lot because I could predict how their sentences would end. I've learnt to do this less as I get older because I know how rude it is, but sometimes I still finish their sentences in my mind and get frustrated as I have to wait for them to stop speaking. As a child, I felt a strange frustration when others couldn't see what I could.

However, heightened intuition comes at a cost. It is a blessing and a curse. Walking into a busy room and picking up on negative energy towards you. Having a social interaction with someone and being acutely aware that you're not their type of person. Sometimes it's better to remain blissfully ignorant of these things. However, it's not an ability I have a choice about – I can't turn it on and off. Plus, neurotypicals (people who have the brain functionality that society considers standard) would call me paranoid.

With every new social encounter or life experience, I gained new information about human behaviour. This information was stored in my brain, which eventually enabled me to spot patterns in this behaviour and predict the likely outcomes.

This ability to recognize patterns meant I could often predict how films would end or who the killer was in a murder mystery. I've learnt not to shout it out in the first five minutes, as it's not a very likeable trait. Spoiler alert: Bruce Willis was dead from the beginning in *The Sixth Sense*.

Getting stuck in decision paralysis

For as long as I can remember, it's amazed me how others are able to make simple decisions with relative ease. When someone asks me to make a decision, my brain shuts down and I'm unable to think.

If someone asks me what I want to eat, I'll forget everything I've ever eaten and not know what to say. If I walk into a supermarket without a list, I'll get overwhelmed by the choice and be unable to make a decision. If I've got lots on my 'to do' list, I find it hard to prioritize. Deciding which task to start first is often so daunting that it causes me to shut down completely.

The most frustrating thing about living with ADHD is when someone witnesses a shutdown and calls me lazy. I get it, it might look like laziness when I'm lying on the sofa, doom-scrolling social media, but the truth is, I'm in a state of decision paralysis and overwhelm.

I know I need to clean the flat. I know I need to renew my car insurance. I know I need to send that email. I know I need to reply to that friend. I know I need to drink water. I know about all these things, but trying to prioritize them is exhausting. I over-analyse everything and end up doing nothing.

The frustration is compounded because people think ADHD means we should all be physically hyperactive (and sometimes we can be – remember that time when we did a week's worth of stuff in an afternoon?), but most of the time it's internalized, it's in my mind, and it causes me huge overwhelm, so please don't call me lazy. It isn't a choice.

Driving

My ADHD makes me a great driver. I can hyper-focus on the road. I'm super-fixated and aware of everything around me. My music's really loud, or I'm singing my lungs out. It's the perfect amount of stimulation and because of this, I find driving really comforting.

My hyper-vigilance means I know exactly what's happening half a mile in front of me and I know what's happening half a mile behind me. I'm constantly checking my mirrors. My sixth sense means I can predict what other drivers are going to do. I've got amazing reflexes, so I can react super-fast when another driver does something stupid.

I get lost easily, so I'm totally dependent on Google Maps. And please don't make me sit in traffic. And if you're a passenger in my car, *please* don't talk to me. But apart from that, I honestly think I'm the best driver I know and my car insurance company should give me a discount.

Oops. I just missed my exit again . . .

Out of sight really does mean out of mind

I live in a constant state of 'now'. I'll try my best to explain what I mean by that. I find it hard to think about something if it isn't directly in front of me. It's the reason why I forget where I've put things. If I can't see something, it doesn't exist.

It's also the reason why I struggle to maintain friendships.

Don't get me wrong, people like you and me absolutely love meeting new people. If a new person is in front of us, we can hyper-focus on that person and spend many hours in deep conversation with them. They're a new source of dopamine and it feels great.

Maintaining a flow of communication afterwards is where the problem lies. Here's what normally happens to me:

1 The new friend sends me a text message.

2 I'll look at my phone.

3 I won't have the mental capacity to reply right now, so I'll tell myself I'll reply later.

4 I get distracted by something else and forget about the text message.

5 A few days go past.

6 The new friend sends me another text message, along the lines of, 'Just checking you're okay and got my last message?'

7 I assume the new friend thinks I'm rude, which flares my rejection sensitivity.

8 I don't have the mental capacity to respond right now.

9 I get distracted by something else and forget about the text message. Again.

10 A few weeks go past.

11 The new friend sends me a text message. It simply says, '???'

12 I'm now too scared to ever speak to this person again.

Before I knew I had ADHD, I would try to remember dates, times and appointments. You don't need to be a rocket scientist to predict how that turned out. My life was chaotic. It was an endless cycle of receiving text messages saying, 'Where are you?' I feel anxious just thinking about it.

By keeping visual reminders of the important things in my life, I've been able to enjoy a much better rate of success in both my friendships and the number of tasks I successfully complete. My whiteboard has been a life changer for me. It sits on my desk right behind my computer. I have lots of different colour board pens that I use to write down tasks.

I invited Eric Whittington (aka Life Actuator) onto my podcast and we spoke at length about this issue. He, like me, struggles to maintain friendships. He explained how, after he moved from one part of America to another, he often went long periods of time without speaking to his family. Not because he didn't love them, but because he often forgot they existed.

When I was speaking with Eric, I was amazed at one of the points he made: he said he often observed other people existing and assumed that that's how everyone must function. For example, when he saw other people seemingly maintaining friendships with ease, he assumed he must be able to do the same, therefore there was no requirement to put any coping strategies in place. As he got older, he realized this wasn't true. His brain was different from those of the people he was observing, so he needed to act in a different way to achieve the same results.

He realized that he wasn't great at keeping in touch with people and that he wanted to get better at it. To fix this problem, he explained how he's now intentional with setting reminders for himself. If you're struggling with this, you can put a reminder in your calendar, you could write on your whiteboard or you could even leave sticky notes on the fridge that say 'CALL MUM', or 'TEXT FRED BACK!'.

These solutions might seem drastic, but if they work for you then they're not silly at all. Writing down thoughts the moment I have them has been crucial for me. If I don't do that, they will disappear forever.

My mind is at its best at night. It's when I'm feeling most creative and 'switched on'. I do myself a favour by using this extra brainpower to plan my tasks for the next day. I'm always very grateful to night-time Alex when I wake up and see the morning 'to do' list I've left myself.

I'm diagnosed. What now?

When you get an ADHD diagnosis, you begin to realize that grief doesn't only mean, 'I've lost something', it can also mean, 'what could have been?'

What could have been if I had known earlier? Maybe that relationship would have lasted. Maybe that friend would still be in my life. Maybe I would have loved myself instead of pretending to be something I wasn't.

Grief is mourning the years of constant confusion, not understanding why I struggled in certain situations or erupted in the face of rejection. Grief is realizing I was playing the game of life on hard mode. I was swimming against the tide and I had no idea.

But there's a saying: the best time to plant a tree was 20 years ago. The second best time is right now. So congratulations to everyone who's received a late diagnosis and has decided to plant their tree at the second best time.

I'll never know what could have been. But what I can do now is turn that grief into gratitude. And be grateful for finally finding out I'm not broken and that I don't need to be fixed. Everything in my past makes sense. My life makes sense. I was always enough.

Reflecting

As I look back on the early stage of my life with the knowledge I have now, I'm able to identify a huge amount of masking. It's glaringly obvious that my outward appearance would often contradict what was going on in my head.

To better understand myself, I invited world-leading ADHD coach Christian Ehmen onto the podcast. Christian has ADHD and I found what he said about masking truly fascinating. He sometimes feels like an alien who is unsure how to behave in social situations. He described masking as 'the act of observing human interactions and then copying the behaviour that occurred within them'.

It makes sense. If you observe a human interaction that doesn't result in that person being called 'too much', you'll store that behaviour in your memory bank, ready to reenact it when you encounter a similar situation yourself.

Mirroring someone you're with is also a form of masking. You might adjust your posture, your tone of voice, your volume (even your accent) to match the person you're talking to.

I recognized a lot of this shape shifting in myself. It makes me tired just thinking about it. Constantly adjusting who you are in order to 'fit in' is exhausting. If someone should say, 'Alex, you have an amazing personality', I feel like responding with, 'Thanks. I made it just for you!'

It also ends up with you having low self-confidence. How can someone be confident as a person if they don't know whether their behaviour is a genuine reflection of their authentic self or an act in order to be likeable in a particular moment? All of this results in you having no idea who you really are.

ADHD isn't exhausting. Pretending you don't have ADHD is.

Healthy ways to begin unmasking

The first step to become an unmasked version of you is to notice why you mask in the first place.

Here are some common reasons for masking:

1 You think being vulnerable will be a burden on other people.

2 You are terrified of criticism so you put on a likeable persona (this persona can change depending on who you're with).

3 You have a deep feeling of being unlikeable so you pretend to be someone else. This feeling can be caused by a childhood of receiving negative feedback in response to your behaviour being different from that of other children.

Deciding to unmask is a very personal decision and one that must be implemented very slowly. It's ultimately a process of self-discovery after years of pretending to be someone else. Unmasking too fast can be dangerous. You might find yourself in a vulnerable position.

For example, unmasking at work has caused people to face bullying and discrimination (more on ADHD at work later). There is no requirement to unmask in all situations at the same time. You might take it further with your partner or a friend and then carry on going to work with your mask still fully on. There's no shame in being inconsistent. You must put your own safety first.

Completing self-awareness exercises is a good way to discover who you really are. (Remember, many people have been masking for so long, they have no idea how to be their true self.) Here's an exercise you can try.

In the evening, sit on the end of your bed and close your eyes. Think deeply about the day that's just passed. Ask yourself the following questions:

1 What happened today that brought me joy?

2 What happened today that made me anxious?

3 What tasks did I enjoy?

4 What tasks frustrated me?

Write down your answers.

This simple task has been very beneficial for me. Over time, it has given me an arsenal of self-awareness that I never had before. It's given me the knowledge required to say 'no' more frequently, and it's given me the confidence to say 'yes' more often. It's allowed me to make decisions that are more aligned to my true interests.

As I say, masking is exhausting. A lot of people go years and years without knowing they're masking and wonder why they feel burnt out all the time. It caused me so much brain fatigue. I can do a day's worth of socializing, but it breaks my brain because it's a constant effort to appear likeable. At the end of the day my brain is *finished*. I have literally nothing left to give. I don't understand how neurotypicals can do the same amount of socializing and still have more to give.

I used to feel a lot of shame about feeling different. It was this shame that made me mask. It was always an effort to camouflage or compensate for my 'weirdness'.

Finding people similar to me has been pivotal in my journey to self-acceptance. Spending time with like-minded people that 'get you', that understand how you think and that you don't feel the need to constantly say 'sorry' to.

> Find people who don't tell you to 'calm down' when you're excitedly sharing a story with them.

> Find people who skip the small talk and jump straight into the heavy stuff.

> Find people who don't ask why you're using a fidget toy.

Finding my tribe has been the most liberating part of processing my diagnosis. I just wish I had found them earlier.

Social media is such a great tool for finding communities of like-minded people. You can easily find groups of neurodivergent individuals, chat with them, share stories and create meaningful connections. A neurodivergent person has a brain that operates outside the realms of what society considers standard. They have different strengths and challenges. Many diagnosable conditions fall under the neurodivergent umbrella, such as autism, ADHD and dyslexia.

I always thought I was weird, but since my diagnosis, my eyes have been opened to another possibility: I'm different from the definition of 'normal' that I was taught and as I'll explain throughout this book, being different comes with amazing strengths.

2

Finding our ADHD strengths (and working out how to use them)

If you Google 'ADHD traits' you will find a list that looks like this:

- Struggle to focus
- Struggle to complete tasks
- Struggle to pay attention
- Struggle with organization
- Struggle with planning
- Struggle with stress.

It's all struggle, struggle and more struggle. It's enough to make anyone feel hopeless.

We can all agree, ADHD has its challenges, but there are loads of *positive* traits, too:

- Resilience
- Creativity
- Excellent problem-solving skills
- Hyper-focus
- Calm in a crisis (some of the most stressful jobs are staffed by those with ADHD)
- Conversational skills
- Spontaneity
- Entrepreneurial
- Empathetic and intuitive
- Thinks outside the box
- Ability to derive patterns where others see chaos
- Courageous
- Ability to find unique solutions to difficult problems
- Ability to talk about different topics at one time
- High energy
- Willingness to take risks.

And that's just the tip of the iceberg.

I have no doubt we can all look back into our past and spot these traits in action. (I know I'm not the only one who's completely calm during an emergency.) It's so easy to forget about our strengths and to focus on the challenging aspects of ADHD. It's why so many of us struggle with imposter syndrome and self-doubt. We literally forget about our accomplishments.

For example, when a neurotypical person accomplishes something (e.g. they get promoted at work or they successfully complete a task), they will store those memories in their brain. They will allow themselves time to reflect on, and be grateful for, their ability to complete the task. They'll also be able to remember that gratitude next time they embark on a similar task, thus enabling them to start the task with more confidence than they had previously.

By contrast, when an ADHD person (me, you, any of the ADHD people we know or love) accomplishes something, they will quickly move on to the next task, and the next, and the next, and so on, without any pause for reflection and gratitude.

While this velocity of accomplishment can be advantageous for us (we are able to get a lot of stuff done in a short amount of time), it can also lead to us experiencing something called success amnesia.

'Success amnesia' is a general term for when someone literally forgets about their success. When I found out about it, I was determined to find a solution to it.

As part of my journey to find that solution, I invited Leanne Maskell, bestselling author of *ADHD: An A–Z*[1] and founder of ADHD Works, onto the podcast. Leanne shared with me some insights and strategies that will forever change how I remember my accomplishments. I've included them for you here.

1 If you can, hire a coach

First, Leanne recommended hiring an ADHD coach. An ADHD coach is a trained professional who understands how to help you manage the challenging aspects of the condition. Having a weekly (or bi-weekly/monthly) session with your coach, who can remind you how great you are, can be really beneficial in countering the effects of success amnesia.

2 Use your journal

Second, Leanne highlighted the importance of journalling. She emphasized how important this simple exercise is and how it can be used to remind you about your success. She writes down her accomplishments every day and on a monthly basis she writes down the bigger monthly achievements. Leanne explained how important it is to use your journal as an Evidence Book. When you're due to start a task and you feel like an unqualified imposter, you can use your Evidence Book to challenge your thoughts.

3 Celebrate your wins

Third, Leanne shared how she makes time in her calendar to celebrate her wins. For example, she will eat out in a restaurant or treat herself to something special. This creates a gap between her accomplishments and builds an association between the achievement and a reward. It also gives her time to reflect on (and be grateful for) her success.

4 Write yourself a letter

Finally, and arguably most importantly, Leanne bravely shared the story of how, during her most vulnerable times, she writes herself a letter in the morning to remind herself how awesome she is.

Thank you, Leanne. I am forever grateful for your wise words.

So, how do I 'embrace my strengths'?

We all have incredible strengths. However, because our world is designed for neurotypical people, it can take longer for us to discover ours.

For example, if we hopped in a time machine and went back 30,000 years to when humans lived in tribes, the traits of ADHD would be very beneficial. Our alertness would make us great hunters. Our high energy and fearlessness would make us great protectors. We would happily stay up all night, stoke the campfire and keep watch over the sleeping tribe.

Today's world, however, caters much less for ADHD. Children are expected to sit in a classroom all day. Adults are expected to sit in an office all day. If we display our natural behaviour, we are called 'too much'.

In fact, kids with ADHD are exposed to 20,000 negative comments by the age of ten.[2]

> 'Calm down!'
>
> 'Stop doing that.'
>
> 'Why can't you just be normal?'

All of this corrective messaging compounds over time to create a person who has a deep feeling of being different. As a result of this, they become experts at pretending to be normal. They alter their personality to match who they're with at any given time.

As a result of this constant shape shifting, they have absolutely no idea who they actually are. Their identity is lost within a lifetime of masking. Consequently, because the person has little understanding of who they are, it becomes impossible for them to identify their own strengths. This results in further feelings of inadequacy and low self-esteem.

How do we break free from this cycle and embrace our ADHD strengths? There are three stages. The first two are:

Stage 1: You must become aware that you're neurodivergent and that you've spent a lifetime pretending to be someone you're not. The fact that you're reading this book probably means you're already at this stage. You've had the liberating realization that there's an explanation for your differences. You were never lazy. You were never 'too much'. You were always enough.

Stage 2: You must begin to understand who you really are. Many neurodivergents have masked for so long that they don't know what's 'them' and what's 'masking'. A lifetime of overcompensating, forcing eye contact and scripting responses to questions has distracted you from building any self-awareness, let alone understanding what your strengths are.

Once the penny drops and you realize there's a beautiful stranger hiding underneath the mask, you can begin to grow your self-awareness. Here are three simple exercises you can try:

1 Study your knee-jerk reactions

All of us will experience things in our day-to-day that immediately fill us with emotion. It could be intense joy, sadness, anger, excitement, anticipation, nervousness, craving, boredom, desire, relief or many other emotions.

It's important to monitor these instant reactions as they often come as a result of something aligning or misaligning with our intrinsic core values. The reaction is instant (and sometimes very intense) because the body's decision to respond bypasses the brain, in the same way your body will jerk your hand away from a source of intense heat without you consciously having to think about it.

For example, if you witness someone dropping litter in the street and you immediately feel frustration or rage towards that individual, that's a strong signal to suggest you find that behaviour disrespectful.

If you feel overwhelmed with happiness immediately after helping someone, that's a strong signal to suggest you're a kind and empathetic person. You literally feel the happiness that you've created in that other person's life, even if it was only for a short moment.

These two examples are here to demonstrate what I mean by a knee-jerk emotional response.

The situations that crop up in your day-to-day life will be unique to you and therefore your knee-jerk reactions will be unique to you. To increase the chances of me remembering my reactions, I try my best to write them down immediately. For example, I have a notepad full of pages that say things like,

'Susan asked me to design a company logo for her new business. That made me feel excited', or 'Eraaj asked me if I'd prefer to work from home today. That made me happy. I'm much more productive when I'm working from home'.

Over time, this notepad fills up with my knee-jerk reactions and it begins to paint a clear picture of my strengths.

2 Ask the people you love

Asking a trusted friend or family member for positive feedback can be a great way to build self-awareness. Ask them questions such as:

'What do you think my strengths are?'

'What do you think makes me happy?'

'When do you think I'm not stressed?'

All these questions can give you a more dynamic view of your own qualities. Our own view of ourselves can often be clouded by thoughts of self-doubt and inadequacy (due to the 20,000 corrective messages I mentioned earlier), so it's essential to hear from a trusted third party who can give you honest praise. It's vital that your trusted person understands rejection sensitive dysphoria (RSD) (I explore this horrid sensation in great depth later) so as to keep their feedback positive and ADHD friendly.

3 Watch yourself, literally

If you really want to know what your strengths are, you should watch yourself when no one else is watching. I don't mean installing mirrors on every wall in your home. I mean being aware of your actions when you're under no pressure to mask.

When I was a little boy, I enjoyed creating stuff. As I mentioned in the introduction, when I was very little I created a board game. I sent my game to as many board game manufacturers as I could. I did all of this when I was alone. When I was at school, I never displayed any of this creativity or entrepreneurialism because I was pretending to be someone I wasn't. I was so busy shape shifting and trying to be likeable that my personality was constantly changing.

My authentic and unmasked self was clearly visible when I was left to my own devices. I can look back now and in between the long periods of masking, I can see myself being myself. I loved to create stuff. I got a huge amount of joy from building businesses. I was an entrepreneur.

My ADHD strengths were hiding in plain sight. But I wasn't paying attention. I was too busy worrying what others were thinking about me. I wasn't watching myself.

The third stage in embracing our ADHD strengths is:

Stage 3: You must ask for your strengths to be accommodated.

In 2016, I worked at a marketing agency. There was loud music, a table tennis table and an office dog. Sounds fun? Nope. Sensory nightmare. The constant 'pinging' noise from the table tennis ball made it impossible for me to focus, not to mention the music and the smell of wet dog farts.

I was hired with high expectations. I was the LADBible guy. So my inability to focus caused me a lot of anxiety, as I knew I wasn't meeting those expectations. I left that marketing agency after two months. I had grown their Facebook following to around 5,000.

Six months later, I joined another agency. But drawing on my last experience, I said:

Please let me work from home sometimes.

Please judge me on my outcome, not my process.

When I'm in the office, please let me work downstairs in the quiet canteen.

But most importantly: please trust me.

They said 'yes'. Three months later, their Facebook following had grown from zero to 8 million.

Simple accommodations can make a huge difference.

My outcomes are consistently high, but my processes are never consistent. One day I might get absolutely nothing done. Another day, I might get four hours of work done at a random time of the day. Another day, I might get 40 hours of work done in four hours. On another day, I might get hyper-focused at 4 p.m. and stay in the office until midnight. ADHD makes my processes unpredictable, but it makes my outcomes outstanding.

Employers should always judge people on their outcomes, not their processes.

How to explain ADHD to your boss

Making the decision to disclose any medical condition to your boss should be carefully considered, with the potential risks weighed against the potential benefits.

For me, the main risk has always been a lack of understanding within the organization, which can lead to discrimination or bullying. In situations like this, I always rely on my intuition to inform me whether or not I'm in a safe environment to disclose my diagnosis or to ask for help.

Is the company putting out signals that suggest they are open and willing to accommodate ADHD? Are those signals genuine or are they simply ticking a box? Has my company brought in neurodivergent speakers and generally made an effort to educate the people within the organization about neurodiversity? Is their website accessible for those with a hidden disability and do they have a clear accommodations policy? Have I witnessed any hurtful communication on the topic of neurodiversity?

Our heightened intuition, combined with the observable evidence, will give us a clear indication as to whether we are in a safe environment or not.

A conversation with a colleague

I once disclosed my ADHD to a colleague and they immediately said, 'Is that why you're late sometimes?' I said, 'Yes, but it's also the reason my intuition can warn you that the person you're having that business meeting with is trying to screw you over.'

I have amazing pattern recognition, which means I'm amazing at predicting future trends.

I'm entrepreneurial, which means I'll think like a CEO and you'll benefit from having another out-of-the-box thinker within your organization.

I've got great conversational skills and I'm a super-fast thinker, which will be an asset to you at any negotiating table.

So yes, my ADHD is the reason I'm late sometimes, but it's also the reason I forget to take my lunch break, so it balances out.

The colleague looked at me in amazement and said, 'That makes a lot of sense.'

ADHD in the workplace can be a massive strength. Unfortunately, too many business owners still think that ADHD is a problem. It's pure ignorance built on old-fashioned stigmas and stereotypes. ADHD can be challenging, but polls show that neurodivergent employees have many strengths, such as creativity, innovation and focus.[3] These strengths, however, are often hindered by a lack of workplace accommodations.

An ADHD mind might think outside the box, spot patterns and trends, spot gaps in the market and find unique and cost-saving ways of solving problems.

Having ADHD minds within your organization will give you a fresh perspective, a new way of thinking and a competitive advantage.

Putting accommodations in place is the best investment a company can make. Those simple accommodations will enable the ADHD mind to deliver results which will make the cost associated with the accommodations shrink into insignificance. It's about time we forgot about old-fashioned, outdated stereotypes and recognize ADHD as a strength in the workplace.

As I've said before, we all have amazing strengths. The problem, however, is that the 'normal' way of living isn't always aligned with the conditions we need in order to thrive. My example above is work related, but the same principle applies for every aspect of our lives. Our work, relationships (more on this later) and everything in between can require a shift from what we all consider to be 'normal'. As I will repeat over and over again in this book: forcing ourselves to be neurotypical will cause us great anxiety, so we must ask the world to accommodate us better.

For me to better understand workplace ADHD accommodations I invited Jodie Hill, a lawyer with ADHD, onto the podcast. Jodie specializes in employment law. She's fiercely passionate about improving the workplace experience for people with ADHD. It was a fascinating conversation in which I gained a huge amount of knowledge that I will share with you here.

First, Jodie made it clear that you don't need a diagnosis to be entitled to workplace accommodations. You simply need to show that your anxiety is substantially affecting your ability to do your job. This can be done through journalling, so you're recording the environment and the challenges, and eventually by asking your doctor for a note.

Jodie said you can ask your employer to allow you to start earlier or later than the traditional time each day. Many neurodivergent people can feel overwhelmed by the rush-hour commute. This results in them being unsettled and anxious for the rest of the day. Allowing you to bypass this overwhelm is a minor accommodation but it will result in you being far happier and more productive.

Many of us, as described in my own experience in the marketing agency, get over-stimulated in busy offices. It's so sad to think how many of us are sitting behind a desk, full to the brim with anxiety, heavily masking and therefore unable to do the job that we're capable of doing.

Jodie explained how you could ask to work from home where there is less noise and fewer distractions. If you need to be in the office, your employer can provide you with noise-cancelling headphones and fidget toys. (I always hold a fidget toy when I'm working or talking on stage. It helps me concentrate.)

Among many other things, we're allowed to ask for ADHD coaching, mini-deadlines to fire up our ADHD brains, written notes after a meeting (my memory is so bad, so this is a life saver), a quiet space to work, a body double (another human with whom to share your space in order to feed off each other's energy), regular check-ins, step-by-step instructions for large tasks, visual reminders for meetings and a map of the building.

Asking for regular breaks is a straightforward way to avoid brain fatigue. Before I knew I had ADHD I never understood how other people could complete the same amount of work as me yet still have more energy to give to after-work activities. I watched in amazement as they planned things to do with their partner or to meet colleagues in the local pub for drinks. My brain was fried after work. I had no energy left for any of this extra stuff.

Since discovering I have ADHD I take regular breaks throughout the day. They help me to recharge my mental battery. This helps me spread my energy throughout the day and be more present after work with my partner.

You will, over time, grow your understanding of how your brain works best. With this greater understanding, you can begin to ask for little changes. For example, I never understood why I felt so anxious after someone asked me for a 'quick chat' without any context. I would overthink, over-analyse and catastrophize. I would be a ball of anxiety until the dreaded 'quick chat' occurred and I was reassured that my world wasn't about to end.

Since my diagnosis, however, I don't allow anyone to cause me this much anxiety. If someone asks me for a 'quick chat', I immediately ask for some context. This enables me to have a stress-free existence until the chat happens.

Additionally, I never understood why work meetings made me anxious. I have many memories of me sitting in meetings and being unable to think clearly enough to contribute. My brain was too busy analysing the situation and worrying about what everyone thought of me. I was terrified someone would point at me and ask me for my thoughts. So I just sat there, silently tapping my sweaty foot against the floor until the meeting came to an end.

Time and time again, the outcome of the meeting was decided by the loudest and most confident voices. I strongly believe, however, that the best ideas are often trapped inside anxious minds. Now, therefore, I always advocate for the following:

- Give everyone all the information that would have been presented in the meeting. This can be done via email.

- Set a deadline (24 hours works well) for everyone to put forward their solutions/ideas. This can also be done via email.

It's a simple change that bypasses so much anxiety.

With great hyper-focus comes a great advantage

One of our biggest strengths is our ability to lose ourselves in focus. We can operate at superhuman levels if we're working on something that excites us. It's very ironic considering the 'AD' in 'ADHD' stands for Attention Deficit. We don't have a deficit of attention. We have an executive function problem. In other words, we're allergic to the boring stuff! (I'll chat more about managing the 'boring stuff' later.)

If I'm interested in a topic, I can write a 3,000-word essay on it at two in the morning. If you ask me to prepare a simple invoice, however, it feels like there are two heavy-duty bricks attached to my pen.

UNILAD, the social media brand I set up when I was 20 years old, was a consequence of hyper-focus. I became obsessed with social media in 2010. That was the year I founded UNILAD from my university bedroom. I only left the room to use the loo, eat and drink. My laptop screen was my entire world. My peripheral vision ceased to exist.

I no longer joined my housemates for the pub quiz. I was euphoric and zoned in. I had found my happy place. It was like someone had turned off all the lights but kept a torch pointed at my computer. My mind was ten steps ahead of my typing. Within three weeks I had created a website and grown the UNILAD following to 1 million.

LADBible was also the consequence of hyper-focus. My TEDx talk was a consequence of hyper-focus. My Mount Everest trek was a consequence of hyper-focus. My marathons are a consequence of hyper-focus. This book is a consequence of hyper-focus.

Our ability to intensely fixate on a project for hours and hours sets us apart from many of our neurotypical peers.

It's important to recognize when you're in a hyper-focus and to know what sorts of activities send you into one. This will build on the self-awareness exercises we explored earlier in this book. We typically hyper-focus on things that intrinsically interest us. By paying attention to what activates a hyper-focus, we can build on our understanding of ourselves.

Hyper-focus is a strength that we must embrace responsibly. (Just don't interrupt me when I'm in the middle of one. There will be rage.)

When to take your foot off the pedal

As described above, hyper-focus can be advantageous. However, it can also interfere with other important areas of your life. (I once spent eight hours in a hyper-focus and forgot to attend my own birthday party.)

Hyper-focus is also the reason people with ADHD are more susceptible to burnout. Before my diagnosis I never understood why I could work intensely for two weeks but then would be unable to get off the sofa for two days. I wanted to learn how to manage burnout, so I invited Kate Moryoussef onto the podcast. Kate is the host of the chart-topping podcast *ADHD Women's Wellbeing*.

It's so easy for people with ADHD to take on too much. Kate shared how important it is to recognize when your body is signalling to you that it needs a break.

Irritability, snappiness and heart palpitations are among the warning signs she looks for. When she notices any of these things, she stops working and takes stock of her current workload. During this pause, Kate asks herself the following questions:

Have I agreed to too many meetings?

Have I over-committed myself?

Am I working late too often?

What can I pull out of?

What can I change?

It's always a good idea to get outside and go for a walk or meet a friend for a coffee. During these periods of early burnout, we should remind ourselves to be more intentional about our choices.

There are many tips I can share that will help you manage burnout: make sure you get plenty of sleep, spend quality time with people away from work, get outside, be active, eat well and practise mindfulness. All of these are great, however there is one bit of advice I wish I could give my younger self: pay attention to the small things because these are always the first to feel the effects of burnout.

The following is a list of examples of 'small things':

- When I feel the urge to burst into tears for no reason.

- When I bite my fingernails too much and make them bleed.

- When I clench my jaw too tight and feel pain in my teeth.

- When things that don't normally send me into an emotionally dysregulated rage send me into an emotionally dysregulated rage, e.g. stubbing my toe.

- When I start ordering take-away food more than normal.

Each of us will have our own list of 'small things'. If you notice any of your 'small things', it might be time to take your foot off the pedal and have some rest. They are early-warning signs I have learnt to respect.

Lean into your ADHD strengths, ignore the noise

Many of the patterns of behaviour that I associate with ADHD (and which have played a huge part in my success) contradict what society says is 'normal'. For example:

- I don't work at 'normal' times.

- I don't complete my work in advance.

- I don't work well in teams.

I've tried to do these three things. I've tried to force myself to sit down and work during the normal nine-to-five slot, but my brain is a stubborn beast that prefers evenings.

I've tried to complete work in advance, but unless it's due tomorrow, I end up on YouTube learning about the unknown mating habits of blue whales.

I've tried to work in teams, but my social anxiety blocks my creativity.

I also don't use organizational tools that are designed for neurotypical people. For most of my life I used the electronic calendar on my phone because that's what I thought adults are supposed to do. This method came with a problem. I always forgot to check my electronic calendar. How am I supposed to remember to check an app on my phone? I can set myself reminders and all of that, but I realized there is another solution.

I have a large whiteboard on my desk. It's the perfect ADHD-friendly calendar. It's big, bright and always directly in front of me. It has colour-coded magnets that really help me stay organized. I used to be ashamed of people seeing it because I thought it looked childish, but now I can't stop talking about it.

I've always been told that my ideas are 'too much' or that I should 'slow down'. For example, when I started UNILAD I had lots of competition. I was eager to push ahead and become the No. 1 Facebook page in the UK. Everyone else was marketing their Facebook page in the traditional way. I, however, decided to think outside the box and started the 'Safe Sex Campaign'.

All my university friends told me the idea was silly. They said I should stick to the traditional ways to promote a business because that's what we were taught in school and that's what works. My creative mind, however, was convinced this was a good idea.

The idea was simple: anyone that followed the UNILAD Facebook page would receive free contraception. I impulsively rushed down to my local sexual health clinic and pitched the idea to them. They loved it. They said a campaign like this was 'much needed'. They gave me two industrial-sized boxes of contraception (I got some funny looks walking home that day) and they agreed to fund the postage and packaging costs.

I announced the campaign the same day. It went viral. Approximately 35,000 students joined the UNILAD Facebook page in 48 hours. The campaign quadrupled the size of the business overnight and it didn't cost me a penny.

Two weeks later I received an email from the largest pizza company in the world. They offered me a significant amount of money in exchange for some promotion on UNILAD. I must have read that email 50 times. My mind was simultaneously in shock and also making the decision to drop out of university. That was the validation I needed. UNILAD was suddenly a viable business model.

I have lots of examples like this and they all have one thing in common: they are all done on impulse. I just 'do' things. I think you have to have ADHD to understand what I mean by this. Society often tells us we need to analyse every possible outcome before we take action. It tells us we need to make a business plan. It tells us we need to be risk averse and to be sensible.

I've spoken to many high-achieving people with ADHD and they also just 'do' things. They impulsively started their business, or they impulsively began guitar lessons and then three years later were a successful professional musician.

Our ability to just 'do' things without worrying too much about the risks is a strength we must embrace. If that 'thing' doesn't work out, then we just 'do' something else, and so on, until we find our 'thing'. We all have one and when we find it, our ADHD brain enables us to obsess over it and become world class in that field.

I'll say it again: many of the patterns of behaviour that I associate with ADHD contradict what society says is 'normal'. Society begs us to be cautious, but people with ADHD are the original hunters. We're doers. We create stuff. We start things.

The moment I stopped trying to be 'normal' was the moment I started to thrive.

3

Money can't buy a new neurotype (how to manage our addictions)

I woke up in the hospital. I had no memory of how I had got there. The nurse approached my bed and said, 'Two members of the public found you staggering in an alleyway. It was 2 a.m. You were alone and clutching a bottle of vodka. As they approached you, you slipped and hit your head on the wall. They called an ambulance.'

As the nurse was telling me this, I felt overwhelming shame and anxiety. It was unbearable. I needed my medication to make it go away. My medication was located in a fridge in the petrol station opposite the hospital. White wine was my preference, but I would have swallowed anything at this point.

My eyes darted from left to right and quickly located the exit. I jumped out of bed and stumbled clumsily towards it. I ignored the nurse's voice as she called, 'Alex, where are you going?' Moments later I was approaching the hospital entrance hall. I staggered towards it and tripped on a rug edge.

I was definitely still drunk.

As I got near the exit, two large men wearing jackets with the word 'SECURITY' embroidered on them stood in front of me. I tried to barge past them, but they gripped my arms and pulled me to the floor. I lay there with my cheek flat against the cold floor and my arms held behind my back for what felt like an eternity. I looked around and made eye contact with a woman as she pulled her child away from the scene. She looked scared. If, by the slimmest of chances, you end up reading this: I'm sorry.

Moments later I was escorted outside. My hospital gown was flapping unflatteringly in the wind as I was led into the back of a police car. As the police issued me with a warning, I noticed two people standing next to the car. My mum and dad were looking at me through the window with an expression of fear and desperation in their eyes.

That was my rock bottom.

How did I get to that point?

I've always been an anxious person. I'm at my happiest when I'm left alone to create stuff. I have a tendency to get really excited about a new business idea, buying the domains, designing the branding, but then losing interest within a few weeks. After I finished school, when I was 18 years old, I impulsively created a website called 'Quick Presents'. My website would recommend gift ideas for your loved ones based on their interests. It lasted three weeks before I lost interest and quit. Next, I created a T-shirt printing business. I quit that one after ten days.

This 'boom and bust' cycle went on for two years. My domain registry was a graveyard of abandoned business ideas. I was so embarrassed because I had excitedly told people about all of them. I dreaded bumping into my former confidantes because I knew I'd have to explain why I had abandoned the idea.

My confidence was shattered. I believed I was a useless human being who couldn't finish anything.

Where to next?

I never intended to go to university. School always made me anxious so I assumed university would be the same. However, after my many failed business attempts, I was beginning to run out of options. I applied and was accepted into Oxford Brookes University in the UK.

I anxiously walked into my first lecture. Everyone sat in a circle and one by one announced their names to the other students. As my turn to speak approached

I felt my heart rate increasing. My mind flashed back to a YouTube video I had watched called 'How to starve a panic attack' in which it said you should breathe in through your nose for six seconds before breathing out through your mouth for a further six seconds. This is great advice, but it was too late. I was past the point of no return. I abruptly stood up and marched out of the lecture theatre. I never attended another lecture.

From heartbreak to a multi-million-pound company

Two weeks later I met someone and romance blossomed. It was a very fast relationship. It was full of obvious ADHD behaviour, which, had I known more about ADHD, I might have been able to manage better. (I have a wonderful chapter later in this book all about ADHD relationships.)

The relationship, however, didn't last long. She broke up with me. We didn't 'have anything in common'. I was devastated. I sat in my room desperately trying to think of a solution to this miserable feeling.

To be fair, she was right. We didn't have anything in common. Yet. She was the editor of the university digital magazine. Maybe, just maybe, if I started my own magazine, it might mean we had something in common? It was going to be a university magazine and the word 'Lad' was trending at the time, so the name UNILAD came to me quite quickly. I ran into my housemate's room and said, 'Mate, what do you think of the name UNILAD?' He looked at me, blew out a puff of marijuana smoke and said, 'Yea that's really cool, man.'

So, with a focus group consisting of one stoned mate to validate my idea, I impulsively bought the domain name www.unilad.com.

Why I never abandoned UNILAD (and LADBible)

Every time I started (and abandoned) a business I unknowingly gained an awareness of how my ADHD brain works. Each business attempt was a 'trial and error' and my subconscious was storing the results.

UNILAD was born at the perfect time. My mind was prepped with an arsenal of self-awareness and tips to help me launch (and maintain) my new venture.

Each and every one of you reading this book will have your own journey of self-discovery to embark on in order to figure out what works best for you. I believe, however, that I've learnt the principles that are relevant to anyone with ADHD and I'd like to share them with you now.

1 WRITE IT DOWN

Our minds work fast. It's why we're very creative, so we should embrace this ability. It can also, however, be a distraction when we're trying to focus on something important for a long period of time. Random ideas, thoughts or questions will come out of nowhere and we will feel compelled to act on them immediately.

For example, I was learning how to make the UNILAD website when suddenly I wondered, 'Is space infinite?' The question consumed my mind and I felt an irresistible urgency to open YouTube, delaying the completion of the website by 3 hours.

We feel this urgency to act straight away because we're subconsciously worried about forgetting the thought. You can bypass this urgency by writing the thought down. I always have a blank piece of paper nearby. If I'm working and a random thought enters my mind, I pick up my pen immediately and write it down. I park it for later. This enables me to stay focused on what I'm doing.

Plus, the 'random thought paper' is fascinating to read at the end of the day. It's a window into your subconscious. It's a journal of the workings of your inner mind. It's a great tool for expanding on your self-awareness.

2 THE 24-HOUR RULE

When someone asks us to do something, we can get very excited and impulsively say 'yes'. The immediate thought of a new project or activity can fill our brain with dopamine. Plus, at least for me, the idea of saying 'no' and letting someone down is the stuff of nightmares. I'm a massive people pleaser, after all.

Ultimately, I used to say 'yes' too much and as a result I became overwhelmed by the sheer number of projects I undertook. Also, most of the time, I lost interest in the project, which meant I had to let the person down anyway. It was a horrible cycle of over-committing followed by under-delivering.

The 24-hour rule allowed me to leave time between the 'ask' and my 'response'. When someone asks me if I'm available to help them with something, I immediately say, 'Thanks so much for asking. Let me check my diary (*whiteboard!*) and get back to you in 24 hours.'

This immediately takes the pressure off, allows me time to process the situation and to decide if I have the capacity to commit to a new project. Fundamentally, it puts a pause between my state of heightened dopamine (in which I am likely to say 'yes' to anything) and my decision. It allows time for the 'new ideas' honeymoon period to pass and for me to therefore make a decision when I'm in a more balanced mindset.

This simple rule has saved me from burnout so many times.

3 (PART 1): ACCOUNTABILITY IS OUR BEST FRIEND

Have you ever wondered why a task feels easier when you know someone is watching you? Or if you know the outcome of the task is going to make someone else happy? For example, cleaning my flat is hard work, but cleaning my friend's flat is easy. I'll enjoy doing it, too.

Our natural empathy and drive to make others happy create a powerful source of motivation because we associate the outcome of a task with how someone else is going to feel.

I became aware of this phenomenon when I started UNILAD and LADBible. I made sure to announce my work commitments to the world. I updated my Facebook status with something like, 'I'm learning to build a website! Can't wait to show you all next week', or 'I'm working on an exciting new section of the website and I'll be launching it tonight!'

This simple technique created accountability because I suddenly had a small group of people (my Facebook friends) who were expecting something from me. I felt like they were 'cheering me on' even though in reality I barely knew most of those people.

You can achieve the same psychological hack by simply texting one person. This could be a family member or a trusted friend. 'Hi [insert person's name here], I need to write 500 words today. Can I show you when I'm finished?' Or 'Hi [insert person's name here], can I send you a picture of my sweaty face after I've spent an hour in the gym?'

Relying on my own accountability has always ended up with me quitting. Creating accountability through another person has always ended up with me succeeding.

3 (PART 2): BODY-DOUBLE YOUR WAY TO THE FINISH LINE

Body doubling is a fantastic way to create accountability. It's when you buddy up with someone and attempt to complete a task together.

For example, sorting out a full email inbox can feel like hell on earth for many people with ADHD. However, the task becomes infinitely easier when you have someone watching you do it. The person could be literally sitting next to you or they could be on a virtual video call with you. The simple idea that someone is with you, chatting to you and distracting you from the overwhelm, will make the task magically doable.

4 TURN EVERYTHING INTO A GAME

We love novelty, right? Tapping into this innate desire for 'fun' by gamifying tasks has enabled me to find excitement where I would normally find boredom.

For example, every time I make my bed, I time myself to see how fast I can do it. I have a piece of paper and pen inside my bedside table that I use to keep track of my best time. It's 58 seconds, by the way.

I hold my breath every time I brush my teeth. I play the 'Gangnam Style' song while cleaning my kitchen. I try to finish before the song ends.

I assign a different number of points to household chores. For example:

Emptying the dishwasher = 10 points

Vacuuming (while pretending to be Mrs Doubtfire) = 7 points

Cleaning the bathroom = 9 points

Remembering to empty the washing machine = 4 points

Emptying the washing machine = 8 points

Picking up the sock I've walked past every day for three months = 10 points

I buy myself something nice every time I reach 100 points.

We crave stimulation and we're allergic to boredom. Use this to your advantage.

Back to the story

I used all these principles to my advantage when I was building my social media brands.

UNILAD grew incredibly quickly. Shortly after I created it, I received a Facebook message from a global pizza company offering me money to promote them. The amount was more than I would earn in a year after graduating from university. I dropped out of university the same day.

I packed up my stuff and moved back in with my parents. I had two computer screens on my desk. UNILAD was on one and LADBible was on the other. There was no stopping me. I did, however, need help.

I met two people and the three of us agreed to work on the brands together. Shortly after this, I was kicked out of UNILAD. My 'baby', my source of dopamine, had been stolen from me.

I remember staring at my computer screen, unable to access UNILAD, paralysed with overwhelm and crippled by anxiety. I was not equipped to handle this situation. None of my known 'hacks' applied here. I stood up, slowly walked to my car, drove to the nearest petrol station and bought a bottle of wine. The cashier asked me how I was. I said, 'I'm great, thank you.'

I drove home and drank the whole bottle in five minutes. It was like I had pressed my brain's brake pedal. My thoughts instantly slowed down. My anxiety, at that moment, had disappeared. I fell backwards onto my bed and stared at the ceiling. All was well. I was euphoric. I was gone.

WHY WAS I DRINKING?

I was terrified of confrontation. So scared, in fact, that I ignored the situation. I buried my head in the sand and drank myself to sleep every night. The intervention happened when my mum found 23 bottles of wine concealed under my bed. We had an urgent family meeting. We agreed it was time to speak to a lawyer.

A week passed before I staggered into the lawyer's office. He could definitely smell the alcohol on my breath. He said, 'You will win this if you choose to fight it in court. You will, however, have to give evidence in the witness box.'

In that instant, my mind flashed forward to a thought of me standing in the witness box. Everyone, the judge, the lawyers, the defendants, the press, was staring at me. I imagined their lawyer saying, 'Alex, do you know the answer to this question?' My mind flashed back to the little version of me that sat in the classroom all those years ago.

I abruptly stood up and left the lawyer's office. I headed towards the nearest shop and bought a bottle of vodka. I woke up in hospital 12 hours later with a nurse looking over me, as I described above.

SIX MONTHS LATER: THE TRIAL

Everyone thought I would break my six-month sobriety during the trial. This was, after all, the event that had caused me so much anxiety.

I was cross-examined in the witness box for five days. It was hard. I had to excuse myself several times to allow myself time to 'use the loo'. I was, in fact, doing breathing exercises in the loo in order to divert a panic attack.

Funnily enough, one of the most stressful moments in the trial was during a lunch break. I went on a walk to find somewhere for lunch. After I had finished eating I noticed my phone had run out of battery. I was totally reliant on my phone's sat-nav to guide me back to the courtroom. I was running through the streets of London asking taxi drivers for directions back to the courtroom. I've always been terrible with remembering directions and I now know that's a very common struggle with us ADHDers.

I was proud of myself for getting through the trial. A further three months passed before my lawyer phoned me. He said, 'Alex, are you on your own?'

'Yes,' I said.

There was a pause. 'You've won everything.'

I fell to my knees and burst into tears. I had won the biggest fight of my life. It was a legal battle, but more importantly, it was the biggest mental health battle I had ever encountered. It nearly killed me, but it also made me a multi-millionaire. So I did what any 29-year-old multi-millionaire would do. I booked myself a trip to Las Vegas to celebrate. After all, I was only drinking to cope with the legal stress, right?

I'd love to tell you what I did in Las Vegas, but I can't remember any of it. I was a shaking wreck when I landed back in England. I was admitted to hospital for alcohol withdrawal treatment. The new tattoo on my arm was infected. *When did I get a tattoo?*

Shortly after this, I went to my first AA meeting where I said the most important sentence I'd ever uttered: *My name is Alex and I'm an alcoholic.*

The frustrating link between ADHD and addiction

I wanted to better understand my attraction to alcohol, so I invited several addiction experts onto the podcast. I spoke with Dr David McLaughlan, a consultant psychiatrist with almost a decade of experience working in mental health. He explained how patients came to him for alcohol detox treatment and how, during that process, he frequently recognized that the individual was living with undiagnosed ADHD.

He went on to explain how, after the patient was made aware of ADHD and a treatment plan was put in place, the patient's use of alcohol significantly decreased. The patients were unknowingly self-medicating their ADHD. For example, if someone struggled to fall asleep at night, they might start drinking heavily in an effort to medicate their insomnia.

The link between ADHD and addiction is complex. We can, however, begin to understand it by examining the chemicals within the brain. Dr McLaughlan explained how people with ADHD often have a deficit of dopamine in their prefrontal cortex. This makes it difficult for them to regulate their emotions or to act out executive functions.

Dopamine and another neurotransmitter called norepinephrine are both heavily involved in the path of physiology to addiction. Therefore, if you have a disregulation or a deficit of these two neurotransmitters, as many people with ADHD do, you are predisposed to becoming addicted to substances that give you dopamine, i.e. alcohol, or one of many other drugs.

Exploring the science further, Dr McLaughlan explained how the prefrontal cortex is the part of the brain that is responsible for decision-making. A well-regulated prefrontal cortex helps people weigh up the pros and the cons and therefore make an informed and safe decision.

The emotional epicentre of your brain is called the limbic system. This is where emotions like anger and lust are processed, and the prefrontal cortex regulates it. In ADHDers, the prefrontal cortex is deficient in dopamine. This creates an unregulated limbic system and makes us more susceptible to pleasure-seeking activities. In simple terms, it makes us extremely impulsive.

One of the world's leading experts on ADHD, Dr Edward Hallowell, has described people with ADHD as having a

Ferrari brain but bicycle brakes. We can rush into making decisions very quickly without much thought about the pros and the cons. This can include hedonistic behaviour such as drinking alcohol, taking drugs or engaging in risky sexual behaviour. In fact, it's estimated that up to 50 per cent of people with ADHD are at risk of developing a substance abuse disorder.[1]

I wanted to learn how to further manage my addiction, so I invited Matt Gupwell onto the podcast. Matt is a neurodivergent professional with over 25 years of lived experience involving ADHD and addiction. I asked Matt, 'If someone is in active addiction and they want to stop drinking, what advice would you give to that person?'

He replied, 'The first step is going to be the hardest. The moment you're able to have a genuine clear thought in which you say to yourself "I am not enjoying this anymore" and "I am no longer in control of this" is the moment you're able to admit to yourself that you're powerless over alcohol.'

How to know if you're powerless over alcohol

Ask yourself the following questions:

When I'm reaching for the bottle, am I doing it because I:

1 Want to drink it?

2 Can't stop drinking it?

The most telling sign of addiction is when we're drinking at the expense of real life.

Is my drinking affecting:

1 My work?

2 My relationship?

3 My friendships?

If you can honestly admit that your drinking is having a detrimental effect on any of the above, it may be an indicator that alcohol is doing you more harm than good.

I want to interrupt these thoughts on addiction for a moment and talk about denial. I never thought I was drinking too much. My drinking had to take me to the depths of hell before I admitted that it was doing me more harm than good.

ADHD creates stubbornness and a resistance to authority that serves me well in many situations. This trait also makes it hard for me to recognize my own liabilities.

If I had asked myself the questions I'm asking you to ask yourself, I would have brushed them off as ridiculous suggestions. The truth was, however, that alcohol was affecting my work, my relationships and my health. My deficiency in emotional maturity created an inability to recognize my own weakness that nearly cost me my life.

If I could jump in a time machine and give myself some advice, it would be to look at my drinking habits more objectively. I didn't believe I was drinking too much. However, if I had looked at the number of units I was drinking compared with the recommended maximum amount, it would have been glaringly obvious that I was struggling.

Tips on how to remind yourself of your 'why'

This one requires a bit of pre-planning, but it's worth the effort. Create a mini-diary listing all the memories you have of feeling hungover. Include details such as how awful you felt, how you felt guilty about letting people down due to turning up late, the effect it had on those closest to you and the anxiety that came with all of it. You can even include little pictures here to remind yourself of the dark places alcohol took you to. This is a very personal diary and is for your eyes only.

It's helpful to glance at this diary in those 15-minute moments of craving as a tool to keep you connected with your 'why'.

The opposite of addiction is connection

I walked away from my conversation with Matt with a clear message: you don't need to stop drinking on your own. Connect with someone if you can. Connect with people who understand and who won't judge you. Connect with people who are invested in the same thing as you are. Building a support network of people you trust, who trust you and with whom you can share your deepest emotions, is the single most important thing you can do in order to stay in active recovery.

If you try to 'do it' alone, the demons will creep back in, at some point life will get too much and it's too easy to default to the old habits. So:

1 Admit it.

2 Connect with people.

3 Keep reminding yourself 'why' you stopped.

4 Pick up the phone before you pick up a drink.

The added benefit of connecting with a community of like-minded people is that it will serve as a constant reminder of your 'why'. This is especially important for us, with ADHD, as we can sometimes forget past experiences and emotions.

You'll hear members of your community share stories of their darkest moments and anecdotes involving the horrors that occurred as a result of alcohol, both of which will allow you to stay connected with your own memories and for you to not drift from step 1, admitting it, and to keep denial and a potential relapse at bay.

Matt shared a story that really highlighted the importance of community. He spoke of someone he knew who had been sober for 24 years. This person drank again and ended up in hospital. When he was asked why he drank again, the person said, 'I drifted from my support community. I didn't think I needed them anymore.'

Final thoughts from my chat with Matt

There's no shame in being an addict in recovery. It's empowering to know you're taking steps to create a better and healthier version of you. An addictive personality and seeking dopamine in unhealthy places is the price that some of us ADHDers pay in return for the vast amount of positives that I speak about in this book.

What to do when your friends say, 'Oh go on, just have one!'

One of the biggest challenges we encounter when choosing to leave alcohol in the past is dealing with the inevitable peer pressure from our friends.

Alcohol is ingrained in our society and because of that, it's the only drug we have to justify not taking. To help prepare myself for these situations, I invited Ruari Fairbairns onto the podcast. Ruari is the founder of www.OneYearNoBeer.com and an author. Ruari explained to me his four-point strategy:

1 Be absolutely resolute on your decision before you walk out of your front door. If you're 'on the fence'

about whether or not to drink tonight, you will inevitably drink.

2 If you've made the decision to not drink, plan something for the following morning that you don't want to miss and ensure you have an exit plan before you enter the drinking establishment. It's easier to announce an early exit if you have a reason to justify it.

3 Most social groups have a 'ring leader', i.e. the person who calls the shots. It's helpful to call this person before the night begins and explain that you're not drinking tonight and you'd appreciate their support. Ruari explained how you only need the support of one person to alleviate the peer pressure from the others in the group.

4 Make a decision about what you're going to drink before you leave the house. If you arrive at the venue without this, your subconscious might panic when the bar person asks what you would like, causing your muscle memory to kick in and prompt you to order your favourite alcoholic drink.

Ruari highlighted how important it is to remember, especially in the early stages of quitting or reducing your alcohol intake, that the craving period lasts for only about 15 minutes. It's important to be resolute in these moments and to remind yourself of your 'why'.

My journey with alcohol always amplified the ADHD struggles and it muted the ADHD positives. When I was drinking, my anxiety, shame and overwhelm were all heightened. A hangover meant I was irritable and more vulnerable to an RSD flare-up.

When I'm sober, my creativity, problem-solving abilities and pattern-recognition skills are increased. Sobriety means I can think clearly and better regulate my emotions and react appropriately when I'm exposed to a perceived rejection. Sobriety means I have more energy to go for a walk and think up great ideas, be more present with my partner, have uninterrupted sleep, have a better memory, be less overwhelmed and experience less anxiety.

Stopping or reducing my alcohol intake was the best thing I ever did. It enabled me to take back control of my ADHD, to suffocate the negatives and allow the positives to thrive.

If I could give the younger version of me another bit of advice, it would be this:

> Alcohol isn't for you. It's not a good mix with your brain type. Some people can drink it and it's okay. Some people can't. There's no shame in being one of the people that can't.

> You have ADHD and that means you can do things lots of other people can't do.

> Focus on those things. Focus on being brilliant. Focus on being you.

> You are enough.

4

Making friends with our worst enemy: rejection

I was four years old when I first felt the pain of rejection sensitive dysphoria. I was at nursery. We had spent the morning cutting potatoes in half, dipping them in paint and using them to create colourful shapes on paper. I was so proud of my masterpiece and naturally excited for my teacher to see it.

I sat patiently with a smile on my face. The teacher approached my table and looked down at my artwork. She said, 'Alex, if you grip the potato like this before you dip it in the paint, you'll get a more consistent spread of paint.'

I perceived her advice as a criticism and burst into tears. Her words instantly made me full up with rage and sadness. I thought my teacher would be proud of my work. My heart broke when she made me feel like it wasn't enough.

The smallest criticism can be devastating for us. A friend might say they're too busy to see us and it feels like we're being punched in the stomach. It's an overwhelming feeling of pain and heartache. A boss might make a tiny correction to our work and suddenly everything inside us collapses. It feels like we're drowning. Sometimes, rage bubbles up.

Whenever possible, we should try not to react immediately – otherwise we may lash out and say something nasty, which we later regret. The intense emotions always pass and we're able to look back on the situation; nine times out of ten the person who made the comment meant no harm and we were being irrational – again. But that doesn't make the reaction any less intense when we're in the moment. The emotional dysregulation is unbearable. In that moment, it feels like we're being attacked and that our world is ending.

It makes us huge people pleasers. We avoid conflict. Sometimes we're afraid to leave the house. We'll hide away, just to avoid the risk of encountering a rejection.

Sound familiar? You're not alone. I have spoken to hundreds of ADHDers in my quest to better understand the condition and every single one of them relates heavily to the above description of RSD. In fact, most of them say it is the most crippling aspect of ADHD. I agree.

RSD, when not understood and managed, can have a devastating effect on our relationships and our overall wellbeing. It's the reason so many of us are perfectionists. (We're so scared of receiving criticism that we overcompensate and outwork our neurotypical peers, which often leads to poor mental health outcomes and burnout.)

It's the reason so many of us have been told 'stop being so sensitive' throughout our lives.

It's the reason we get so fired up when someone tells us to do something that we were already planning on doing.

It's the reason we think everyone talks about us behind our backs.

It's the reason we felt rejected when there wasn't a rejection.

Where does RSD come from?

Scientists are divided over whether rejection sensitive dysphoria is a response from the brain's frontal lobe (the part of the brain that I discussed in the previous chapter, which is deficient in the neurotransmitters required to properly regulate emotions) or a response from the brain as it remembers a trauma.

I'm inclined to believe it's both. Here's the thing: we *are* different. And this repeated internalized feeling of being different creates thousands of micro traumas throughout our early lives.

> Why can't you just remember?
>
> Why can't you just be on time?
>
> Why are you being weird?
>
> Just plan your time better!
>
> You're just being lazy.
>
> Stop being so clumsy!
>
> Stop making excuses.
>
> Your room is a mess!
>
> You're so careless.
>
> Stop being odd!
>
> Stop fidgeting!
>
> Pay attention!

Simply writing rejection that list made me feel emotional.

Our ADHD personality traits often don't match up with society's expectation of how a 'normal' child should behave; therefore, we are repeatedly criticized and rejected by our peers. We're continuously told we're odd and that makes us feel broken.

We're not broken. We are, however, haunted by the memory of past criticisms. The memory is embedded in our subconscious. We don't even know it's there. When we encounter a criticism or a rejection as adults, our subconscious is snapped back to the horrible memories of those 20,000 negative messages and we instinctively react defensively.

It's automatic, instant and not our fault. Repeat after me: it's automatic, instant and not our fault.

Why is it not our fault? Because we never intentionally did any of the stuff we were criticized for. None of us intentionally forgot stuff, turned up late or made excuses. None of us was intentionally careless, clumsy or lazy. None of us intentionally lay on the sofa all day, stuck in decision paralysis because we knew how many tasks we needed to do but were unable to prioritize them and therefore did nothing all day.

Being in a constant state of overwhelm wasn't a choice. So how dare someone criticize us for being 'odd' when we were trying so damn hard just to appear normal. We didn't know we were swimming against the tide.

We take the first step towards managing RSD when we accept that RSD isn't our fault. I used to hate myself and carry so much shame when I had an RSD flare-up. I was convinced I was inherently broken. My internal monologue was unbearable:

'My partner must think I'm so childish.'

'I feel so embarrassed about causing a scene like that.'

'Why did I burst into tears in the supermarket?'

All of these thoughts compounded over a lifetime to create a deep fear of confrontation. I was afraid of anything that might trigger a flare-up.

Even when I acquired the new knowledge that it wasn't my fault, it's fair to say that RSD was ruining my life. I wanted to learn how to manage it, so I chatted to Dr David McLaughlan, leading ADHD psychiatrist, about it.

He explained that it's totally understandable to associate being neurodivergent (and therefore growing up feeling different) with an exposure to an increase in early criticism and rejection. Society is not always kind; other kids can be mean, especially when there's a child that appears to act differently. There's a real risk of that child being ostracized in the playground or bullied. Being ostracized, in a child's mind, is the biggest rejection of them all.

David believes those early experiences of rejection prime that person to be more vigilant and to anticipate further rejection throughout their life. Consequently, in order to avoid the pain that comes with a rejection, that person will take steps to avoid it.

This hit me like a ton of bricks. I have always taken steps to avoid rejection. I've always been scared of anyone thinking badly of me, so I have always bent over backwards to please everyone, even when that meant ignoring my own needs.

I often found myself in situations I didn't want to be in simply because I didn't want to offend the person who asked me to be there.

I often found myself ignoring my intuition and being too afraid to say what I thought because I didn't want to encounter an argument.

I often found myself taking on too much work because I didn't know how to say 'no' when someone asked me if I was able to start a new project.

I often felt anxious when I did put myself first because I had this internalized feeling that someone wasn't happy with me and that I was being hated on.

All of these things caused me to become anxious and overwhelmed. It was so hard to simply say 'no' to things.

How I created boundaries and became a 'let me think about it' person

Being a people pleaser was burning me out. It was causing me to have fragile relationships because it meant I was never truly honest with those close to me. I had no self-identity because my identity was always shifting depending on who I was with.

I was becoming frustrated because I could never 'stand up for myself' or assert any clear boundaries. This further impacted my ability to love myself and to have any self-confidence.

There was a lot of in-built shame and fear around setting boundaries for myself, so I knew I had to start small, and I had to start slowly. Here's the first thing I did: whenever someone asked me to do something, I would stop myself from responding immediately. This was deeply uncomfortable because my knee-jerk reaction whenever someone asked me to do something was to immediately say 'yes'.

The uncomfortable feeling disappeared when I filled the silence with 'let me think about it'. I wasn't ready to use the word 'no' just yet. That was too scary. Saying 'let me think about it' felt easier because it was neither a 'yes' nor a 'no' and therefore gave me breathing space to process the decision without triggering my fear of offending the other person.

As I said 'let me think about it' more often, I realized that absolutely nobody had a problem with me saying it. In fact, it was always well received. People respected my ability to put space between their 'ask' and my decision as to whether or not to do it. I was able to think about the 'ask' in my own time and therefore decide what I intrinsically wanted to do. This boosted my self-confidence because it enabled to feel more connected to my true identity.

If I decided I didn't want to do the 'thing', I sent a text message (I wasn't at the stage to say 'no' in person yet) saying, 'Thank you for asking me to do *the thing*. Unfortunately I don't have the time right now, but thank you for asking.'

I purposefully didn't include lots of unnecessary niceties such as 'I'm so sorry but I can't . . .' or 'I'm so sorry to bother you' (unless it was someone I was close to) because we have a tendency to over-explain ourselves and this is a form of people pleasing. My messages were short, polite, to the point.

This might seem like a baby step to many, but for my anxious, over-committing, people-pleasing ADHD brain it was a huge milestone in my journey to setting boundaries and establishing self-confidence.

My life changed when I realized that 'let me think about it' was a complete sentence.

How I went from 'let me think about it' to 'no'

First, I want to say that I'm still not consistently able to immediately say 'no' all the time. I still frequently resort to the 'let me think about it' technique. I've found a great deal of peace in this as I now understand that my fear of rejection is not my fault and that there's no shame in not being perfect all the time.

It's still deeply uncomfortable when someone asks me to do something; however, I've found serenity in those moments because I'm aware that I'm actively taking steps towards setting boundaries. This in itself is massively therapeutic and helpful in progressing our journey towards saying 'no' more often.

Whether or not I say 'let me think about it' or 'no' is very dependent on how I'm feeling in that moment. I'm more likely to say 'no' if my day has been good and I'm feeling emotionally regulated. When those moments happen, I make sure I immediately write down a summary of the moment. For example, if you're at work and someone asks you if you have time to help them with something and you say 'no', making a diary note of that moment will help you remember that point in time and enable you to meditate and reflect on it.

When you reflect on those moments and meditate on them, over time your subconscious will recognize that nothing bad happened as a result of you saying 'no'. This will give you more confidence to repeat that behaviour and to further create more journal entries of positive experiences of you saying 'no'.

Ultimately, we learn that saying 'no' doesn't result in a bad outcome. In fact, the opposite occurs. We become more confident human beings, we become less anxious, we gather more respect from our peers, we have healthier relationships and, most importantly, we become acquainted with our self-identity.

Learning how to manage RSD

We can take steps to shield ourselves from the horrible effects of RSD, but it's not always possible to avoid a flare-up. If someone isn't responding to me with noticeable enthusiasm, I automatically think they hate me.

RSD, for me, is the most damaging trait of ADHD. It's an unpredictable beast that can cause problems in our relationships, friendships and at work. For example, two years ago, faced with a quiet evening, my partner and I were excited to make pancakes. We got in the car, drove to the shops and bought the ingredients to make a feast. The dopamine was flowing and the night was teeming with positive vibes.

We arrived back home, unpacked the bags and began to prepare the pancake mix. I poured the milk into a mixing bowl and cracked two eggs into the milk. I was just getting ready to add the flour to the mix when my partner grinned and said, 'Why have you added the ingredients together in the wrong order? I think you're supposed to add the flour and milk together first and then add the eggs later on.'

I immediately felt every ounce of happiness leave my body. It was replaced with an overwhelming feeling of rage. 'What do you mean?' I said.

'You've added the ingredients together in the wrong order,' she replied calmly. 'The flour will clump together and make lumps if it goes into the mix last.'

Without a moment's pause, my voice raised and I snapped, 'It doesn't matter what order the ingredients go into the bowl!'

The atmosphere immediately shifted. The positive vibes evaporated in a heartbeat. A harmless comment about my pancake mix had triggered my RSD and ruined the night.

I wanted to learn how to control these flare-ups, so I invited Dr Samantha Hiew PhD on to the podcast. I started my conversation with Samantha with a description of how I felt when I experienced an RSD flare-up. I said, 'I'll get a small rejection and I'll feel terrible for days. I'll feel intense sadness or rage. I'll think about it for months. It might pop into my head years later and I'll feel terrible again.'

I asked Samantha what I could do to alleviate the intense feelings. She explained how there are short-term strategies and long-term strategies. Starting with the short-term strategies, Samantha recommended I try to snap myself out of the intensity by forcing my brain to think about something else. For example, biting down on frozen ice would snap my mind out of the emotional intensity and into the 'here and now'.

If you're entering a situation that you know comes with a risk of encountering a rejection, it's a good idea to come prepared with something with a sharp taste, such as a lemon sweet, that you can chew when you feel an RSD flare-up brewing. A lemon sweet is one example, but it must be something that works for you. Every one of us will have our own individual idea of what is a strong enough taste to snap us back into the 'here and now'.

Samantha and I agreed that the most effective short-term strategy was to simply call a friend. This should be a compassionate and trusted friend who can reassure you that the intense feelings you're currently experiencing are valid, but who can also reflect back the reality of the situation and tell you that you're going to be okay. They can tell you all your positive qualities, all the positive things you have achieved and make you feel good about yourself.

Moving on to the long-term strategies, we spoke about why it's important to look within yourself to examine why you react very intensely when confronted with a rejection.

> Did someone make you feel worthless a long time ago?

> Are you working really hard to maintain your self-worth to compensate for that early experience of feeling worthless?

> Do you feel that your self-worth is at stake when someone criticizes you because you have associated your self-worth with how others perceive you?

If your entire self-worth is built on your outward projection and how you think others think about you, then of course you're going to crumble when someone criticizes you. A lot of us were never taught how to feel strong in ourselves without using other people to validate us. We were never equipped with the scaffolding to keep us strong and steady when others said negative things about us.

Over time, the answers to these questions can be discovered through therapy. Therapy can help us build a sense of belief and decondition us from our need for external validation to feel worthy.

RSD in relationships

Samantha and I spoke about whether or not you should discuss RSD with your romantic partner. While we agreed it was a good idea to lay everything on the table, we also agreed that RSD was only one part of ADHD and all the positives should be discussed too. After all, the part of our brain that makes us sensitive to rejection is the same part that makes us extremely loving and empathetic.

We are sensitive. We have inherited a nervous system that is prone to stress and executive functioning challenges. We have increased sensitivity to the world because we hear more, we see more and we feel more. It helps us see things that no one else sees. It helps us empathize and fight for the people we love. We are loyal and we will never leave them behind.

But with this great power comes great responsibility. That responsibility is to manage the emotions. It's a growth process that starts with awareness, compassion and maturity.

Be kind to yourself and know that what makes you sensitive to rejection is the same thing that enables you to connect with people in special ways.

How biology affects psychology

Your ability to manage RSD will also be influenced by your hormonal cycles (men and women alike). This is extremely important to know because without this information, you will unfairly beat yourself up for struggling more at different times of the day or month.

Samantha explained how a woman's monthly menstrual cycle and a man's daily testosterone cycle influence their ability to regulate their emotions. For women, she likened it to having four seasons of the year but within a single month: spring, summer, autumn and winter. During the spring and summer, a woman is in the ovulatory phase of her cycle and is therefore more likely to feel happier, have more energy, be able to sleep better and be able to verbally articulate her emotions. In contrast, during the autumn and the winter there is a decrease in oestrogen, progesterone and serotonin. She may have trouble sleeping, feel slightly depressed and be less verbally articulate. Samantha explained how, during this phase, a woman's memory may be affected, which means her day-to-day life might be more chaotic.

For men, the testosterone cycle happens on a daily basis. The testosterone goes up in the morning and gradually decreases throughout the day. As your testosterone levels drop, you may find yourself less happy and less able to regulate your emotions. This is when you're at a higher risk of reacting badly to a rejection.

It's vital that everyone has an awareness of how biology affects psychology because we can all begin to be kinder to ourselves. Our coping mechanisms might not always work and that's okay. It's not your fault.

Alcohol and RSD is a recipe for disaster

All of my most regrettable RSD flare-ups have happened when I've been drinking. Alcohol strips away my defence mechanisms and increases the likelihood of me reacting explosively to a rejection. I've lost count of the number of times I've woken up alone in the spare bedroom.

Most of the methods for managing RSD include an immediate 'stop and pause'. It's an intentional break between the stimulus and the reaction. Alcohol increases my impulsivity and therefore decreases my ability to apply the 'stop and pause'. It also significantly impacts my sleep quality, which means I am grumpier and therefore less able to regulate my emotional responses.

Every person I've spoken to on the podcast has said lowering their alcohol intake has vastly improved their ability to manage the annoying parts of ADHD, especially their RSD.

Give me a minute, please

When RSD hits us, it hits hard. Rather than reacting impulsively in the moment, train yourself to make 'give me a minute, please' your default response. After this, be ready with a prepared reason to remove yourself from the situation. For example, if you experience a flare-up at work, you could say you need to use the bathroom or you need to get some fresh air. It's completely normal if you need to lock yourself in the toilet cubicle and simply cry. There's no shame in this. It's also completely normal if you need to go outside and pace up and down the street. Again, there's no shame in this.

When you remove yourself from the situation, you're putting space between the stimulus and your reaction. This gives your brain time to regulate itself and to not be influenced by the intense feelings.

The pause also allows you to practise self-compassion. It's a great time to remind yourself that the intense feelings you're experiencing are a symptom of ADHD and not a personal failing on your part.

It's not your fault.

You can also use the pause to communicate with your trusted person who can remind you of your strengths. They can speak with you while you process the situation. If your trusted person is not available, you can give yourself positive affirmations from memory or by reading a pre-prepared list of personal qualities. For example:

I am a caring person.

I am a loyal partner.

I am a creative thinker.

I am intuitive.

I am honest.

During the pause, it's also really useful to ask yourself the following question:

Am I reacting to what just happened or has what just happened caused me to react to something that happened in my past?

Repeat this question in your mind three times. As you repeat it, imagine a bird flying over your head. It glances at you as it glides past. Now imagine a plane flying through the sky above. Imagine a passenger looking out of the plane window. The bird is too small for them to see.

Now imagine an astronaut looking out of the window of the International Space Station. They're just about able to see the plane; it's a tiny white dot moving across their view of planet earth. You can zoom further out with every new thought until you are as far away from planet earth as your imagination can take you.

I find this thought exercise very useful because it:

1 Takes the focus away from the intense feelings.

2 Adds perspective and proportion to those feelings.

It's easy to become overwhelmed and totally consumed with intense feelings. When you zoom out and add perspective and proportion to them, you remove some of the power they have over you. It enables you to take back control of the moment.

Combining this newfound control with the realization that you are not reacting to what just happened, but reacting to an ancient memory which has been recalled by what just happened, gives you a powerful ability to respond in a more proportionate way.

If you're unable to put a pause between the stimulus and the reaction (because we're all human and our impulses will get the better of us sometimes), you can mitigate the consequences by using sentences that start with the word 'I', instead of the word 'You'.

If someone triggers you and you respond aggressively with a 'You' statement (e.g. 'You're wrong!' or 'You have no idea what you're talking about'), the other person will feel unfairly attacked and is more likely to respond with another negative comment. This will further flare your RSD and risk you falling into a spiral of intense negative reactions. This can look like you rage-quitting a job or rage-ending a relationship.

By responding with 'I' sentences (e.g. 'I feel unfairly treated' or 'I don't agree with what you said') you're asserting your boundaries while also avoiding escalating the situation into a full-blown RSD flared confrontation.

An easy way to remember the stages of RSD management is using the acronym: RSD (I told you it was easy to remember!):

> The R stands for Recognize.
>
> The S stands for Stop.
>
> The D stands for Distract.

1 Recognize when someone has triggered you.

2 Stop yourself from reacting immediately.

3 Distract yourself to bring perspective to the situation. Do this either by calling a trusted friend or by doing thought exercises or affirmations.

Come to your senses

I also found activating all five of my senses really helps me to distract myself from the intensity of an RSD flare-up. Immediately after I've been triggered I focus on:

5 things I can see

4 things I can touch

3 things I can smell

2 things I can hear

1 thing I can taste.

This helps me to pull my brain away from the immediate stress and direct it towards a distraction.

If you haven't got anything to taste, become aware of the natural taste in your mouth. If you haven't got anything to smell, smell a piece of your clothing. If you can't hear anything, chatter your teeth together and listen to the noise they make.

During this process you can repeat to yourself: this will pass. I have got through this before. This can't hurt me. This isn't my fault.

Assume their intentions are good

My RSD flare-ups used to be really bad because my default reaction was to think the other person was intentionally being nasty. It helps to assume the other person may, in fact, have an innocent reason for behaving in the way that you perceived to be a rejection.

For example, if someone jumps the line in a supermarket, rather than feel enraged because they have blatantly ignored your existence, imagine they are extremely anxious and in a hurry to buy flowers for their ill relative who's dying in hospital with only moments to live. Or if you're making pancakes and you mix the ingredients in the wrong order, maybe the person who made the perceived criticism is trying to bond with you by giving you a cooking class.

Ultimately, I've found it really useful to reframe every RSD encounter as being a bit of feedback about a very particular part of me and not a criticism or a rejection of the whole of me. Also, it's massively beneficial to recognize that you don't have all the information and that sometimes there is an innocent reason behind somebody doing something that you thought was a rejection.

Of course, you will encounter nasty people who will cut in line and who will insult you, but it's helped me to try to default to giving people the benefit of the doubt, rather than defaulting to assuming everyone is nasty; when you do encounter a nasty person, it's normally always a reflection of their character flaws and not yours.

Each and every one of us will recognize the horrible feeling that RSD brings. It feels like we're drowning. It's an insufferable feeling of heartache and pain.

Clench your fists. Scream at the wall. Cry. It's okay to feel those feelings. Embrace them. But also know that they don't define you. They are not you. They are a flashback to something horrible that happened a long time ago. They're a memory of being criticized for being different, rejected for being weird and ostracized for not being neurotypical.

None of those things is our fault. We are neurodivergent and we have our own unique strengths.

What makes us sensitive to rejection is also what makes us kind, loyal and empathetic. It's okay to have big feelings.

It's what makes us risk takers, entrepreneurs and problem solvers.

We are powerful. We are not alone.

We have ADHD.

5

Our love languages

'I'm breaking up with you Alex. You never listen to me.'

I was sitting in the passenger seat of her car when she told me she didn't want to be with me anymore. We had been discussing our plans for Christmas moments before. I suggested we spend it with my family.

I felt the camel's back breaking as she abruptly pulled the car into a layby. She angrily reminded me that we had been discussing our Christmas plans earlier that day and that we had talked about spending Christmas with her family. She also reminded me that it was the sixth time we had had that conversation.

To her credit, this wasn't an isolated incident. It was a culmination of two years of her feeling like I didn't listen to her. I mean, who could blame her? Here's a list of common occurrences.

I'd ask her what she wanted for dinner, drive to the supermarket to buy it and then immediately forget what she asked me to buy her. She would ask me to clean the bathroom. I would say 'yes'. The bathroom was still a mess when she arrived home from work. She'd tell me she had put a load in the washing machine and to empty it when the cycle had finished. I forgot. The machine was full of damp washing when she came home from work.

'Did you hear what I just said?' was a sentence spoken daily in our house.

I was never able to organize stuff in advance. Valentine's Day always consisted of me rushing down to a petrol station in the morning to buy a bouquet of roses. We spent her first birthday together in a pizza restaurant that had really bad Google reviews and a two-star food hygiene rating but was the only place accepting last-minute reservations.

It wasn't just my inability to remember things that grated away her ability to love me. I took on the role of organizing our finances. I often opened letters from our energy supplier that said we had forgotten to pay the bill and it had therefore doubled. I often opened letters informing me that I had forgotten to pay a parking fine and it had therefore doubled.

A human being's patience and understanding (or lack of in this case) can only stretch so far. She gave me lots of chances to 'sort myself out'.

I was also getting frustrated at my inability to remember dates and conversations. We both thought I was lazy and incompetent. Neither of us understood what we were dealing with. Ultimately, we were judging my ability to be a respected and loving partner on society's expectations of what one should be like. But I wasn't typical. I had ADHD. I was neurodivergent. I just didn't know this at the time.

She drove me back to our flat. I packed my bags and ordered a taxi. She looked at me with shining eyes and said, 'Goodbye, Alex.'

History had repeated itself again. That was the fourth failed relationship that ended with 'you never listen to me' just before the final curtain. If there were an encore, it would consist of my ex walking back on stage and shouting, 'You've forgotten our anniversary, *again*?'

I cried when I received my ADHD diagnosis. Every failed relationship suddenly made sense. None of those arguments was my fault. None of them was her fault. They all happened because the relationships lacked a basic awareness of neurodiversity.

I wish I could go back in time and give myself the contents of this chapter.

I wish I knew people with ADHD might express their love for someone in unique ways.

We might send our partner a love song where the lyrics perfectly articulate how we feel because communicating might be hard, but the song does it so well. Do we really love someone if we don't regularly info dump with them? This is where we excitedly share a large amount of information about a highly focused subject or passion at one time, usually at great detail and length. This is how we demonstrate our trust for someone. This is how we show we want to form a bond.

We want to parallel play and body double with our partners. We want to hug them until it feels like our bones are crushing. We want you to crack our back until it feels like our soul is leaving our body.

When you share a story with us and we immediately share a similar story back, it's not because we think our story is better, it's because we were listening and we want to show you that we relate. This might sound weird to some people, but this is how we form a bond.

Whether you have ADHD or you're dating someone with ADHD, it's important to have awareness of the unique ways ADHD can show up in your relationships. The ADHD brain often has executive function struggles which mean date nights might be difficult to plan, anniversaries might be forgotten and that thing your partner told you they liked and were secretly hoping you bought them for Christmas might be forgotten about.

Most people's expectation of 'love' is for it to be shown in the traditional way: long, heart-felt conversations, romantic dinners and well-planned surprises. Here's the thing: all three of those make me anxious. I'm not good at long conversations, I get fidgety during long meals and I'm not great at planning things.

Let's talk about some of the ways I prefer to demonstrate my love.

Info dumping

Info dumping is when we share a lot of information about our special interest. For example, my special interest is 'social media', so when there's an update to the algorithm, I love to share this with my partner. I explain every single detail. It can sound like I'm speaking at breakneck speed, but she appreciates that because her mind works in a similar way to mine and a slower pace would frustrate her.

This is my preferred conversation style. I'm allergic to small talk. I find it really hard because small talk is essentially a game of table tennis where one person says a sentence or two and then the other person says a sentence or two. My brain doesn't like to switch tasks like this. I prefer to think of communicating as a single task and then listening as another task.

During small talk, these two tasks swap too quickly and I become overwhelmed by the pace. This makes me anxious. I become acutely aware that I'm overwhelmed and worry that I'll say something unrelated or silly when it's my turn to talk.

Info dumping, however, allows me to speak continuously until I've said everything I wanted to say. The other person can then speak continuously until they've said everything they wanted to say. This means we don't have to continuously task switch and deal with the anxiety that comes with that.

In a relationship, it's important to be aware of how each of you prefers to communicate. Otherwise, the ADHD person might begin to mask their true self and try to engage with their partner in the style of a neurotypical. This will cause the masking partner to become anxious and forget key parts of the conversation, which will result in conflict because the other person will assume they weren't listening. The ADHD partner will also be exhausted by the extra effort involved in simply trying to appear 'normal'.

True love and compatibility happen when both people appreciate how the other likes to communicate and they accommodate their preferred style.

We might have stayed up all night obsessively researching a new topic and be extremely excited for you to wake up so we can share it with you.

A safe space is created when we feel able to info dump without judgement. A safer space is created when we know our partner genuinely loves to receive our info dump and even reciprocates with their own info dump. The info dump can happen at any time. Our need to express ourselves is not bound by the traditional framework of activity-based communication. For example, communicating during mealtimes or when we arrive home from work might be considered 'normal'. However, the ADHD person might be brain frazzled during these times and prefer to sit in silence.

In my previous relationships I forced myself to communicate during these times. I had no awareness of ADHD and didn't know I needed some quiet time after work to enable me to transition between activities. I masked, which took even more energy from me, and I became irritable and snappy. Many arguments would have been avoided if I had known what I know now.

Our info dump might come at an obscure time of the night because our energy levels are very unpredictable. Our poor impulse control makes it hard for us to contain it, which is why we can unleash a wave of knowledge onto our partners at unpredictable times of the day or night.

The most beautiful thing happens when your brain energy matches up with your partner's and you info dump with each other for hours and hours. You appreciate the other's style of communication and you thrive when listening to your partner release their thoughts. You stay up all night explaining to each other everything there is to know about the universe, or dog breeds.

Sometimes, of course, one partner will have an urge to info dump but the other person's energy isn't in sync.

When this happens, it's useful to have a safe word that the non-willing partner can use to communicate their position without triggering an RSD flare-up in the other. For example, the non-willing partner could say, 'Love you, but I'm frazzled right now.'

When this happens, the willing person can still info dump onto a piece of paper or use a laptop to type their thoughts. The non-willing person can read this when they're feeling more energetic and the willing person won't feel rejected.

The content of an info dump might be fleeting and that's okay. True love recognizes that their partner might obsess over a particular topic but also have zero interest in it the following day. It's very common for us to get excited about something but move onto another interest moments later. Let's say you and your partner have stayed up all night sharing facts about the universe. When you next communicate with them, rather than assuming they're still interested in the universe, it's a good idea to begin the communication by saying, 'Are you still into the universe?' This gives them the opportunity to tell you if they're still fixated on that topic or if their brain has moved onto another hyper-obsession.

So many of us are used to feeling shame because we have lost interest in something after we have told our friends and family about it. 'Alex never finishes anything he starts' is a phrase that comes to mind. The ultimate love language is when your partner recognizes that trait and makes you feel shameless when your latest obsession has fizzled out.

Body doubling: the echo of two hearts

Body doubling is the act of performing a task with somebody else. The other person could either be helping you or simply keeping you company. This creates a strange but extremely effective type of accountability that helps us start and finish tasks. The other person could be with you 'in person' or with you virtually via a webcam. I like to call it: being alone in company.

In the past, I have asked a friend to come over to my flat simply to give me the motivation to clean. It sounds weird, but if you have ADHD, you'll know what I mean.

Romantic body doubling can look like:

- being with your partner as they empty the washing machine
- being with your partner as they brush their teeth
- being with your partner as they create an invoice
- being with your partner as they take a shower
- being with your partner as they make the bed
- being with your partner as they clean
- being with your partner as they cook.

We act differently when we know we're being watched. We feel a subconscious desire to please the other person and this gives us the motivation to do a task that we would otherwise find extremely challenging.

A friend once explained to me that he found brushing his teeth and showering to be the hardest part of his daily routine. He explained his struggles to his partner (she had the same struggles) and they agreed to do these activities at the same time. One of them would brush their teeth while the other had a quick shower. They would then swap places. He said it didn't work 100 per cent of the time but it massively improved their personal hygiene routine.

He showed me a Valentine's Day card he had received from his partner and she had written, 'You're my lifelong body double.' I thought it was the most romantic thing I had ever seen.

Having ADHD means we're really good at thinking about starting things but really bad at actually starting things. We often lack the self-accountability required to begin tasks – and that's okay! We have issues with executive function and that's not our fault.

Body doubling is the greatest ADHD hack out there. The other person doesn't even have to do anything other than be with you. This gives us the accountability we need to feel motivated. Nothing says 'I love you' better than offering yourself as a body double for your partner.

When my partner is away, there's a high chance I won't be doing any household chores. (Until they send me a text saying 'I'll be home soon'. That always kicks me into action.)

Whispering to your partner that something is urgent so they get it done

People with ADHD thrive on urgency. In fact, we often find it impossible to do a task unless we know it's urgent. In other words, if there's a piece of work that's due in four weeks, we will struggle to start it because the deadline is very far away.

A strong display of affection is to create a sense of urgency in the ADHD partner. This demonstrates that you understand how their brain operates and are happy to help them manage it. For example, if the ADHD partner has a piece of work due in four weeks, the other partner could create lots of mini-deadlines in between now and the final deadline. This will help the ADHD partner feel less stressed as the main deadline approaches.

The mini-deadlines can be made to feel more impactful if there is a real reward after completion. This could be a gift, such as a voucher for a 20-minute head scratch, or a link to a song in which the lyrics perfectly explain how perfect they are.

I love you, please drink water

Finding fun ways to remind the ADHD partner to drink water is a lovely show of affection that will always be appreciated. You could leave sticky notes in their room or on the fridge. You could send them a text message at random times throughout the day.

We can lose ourselves in a hyper-focus for hours and forget to eat or drink. A physical interruption (i.e. you tapping me on the shoulder and reminding me to drink) might cause me to feel upset or angry; however, an indirect reminder such as an email or a text message will prompt me to think about it while also reminding me how much you care about me.

Accepting our impulsive displays of unmasked love

Impulsivity is a huge part of ADHD and it plays a big role in how we show our love for someone. Our displays of love might be spontaneous and unpredictable. One minute, we could be lying on the sofa, doom scrolling social media, but the next minute we've jumped off the sofa and we're ready to embrace and kiss you.

Having ADHD also means that ideas might come into our minds that cause us to instantly jump up and say something like, 'Let's drive to the shops now!' or 'I think it would be fun if we went to the arts and crafts shop and bought the stuff to make a kite.'

It won't always be possible to accommodate these impulses because, as you know, the ADHD urge to start new hobbies is sometimes expensive and often short lived. It is lovely, however, to lean into the quirkiness and embrace the impulse together.

This show of impulsive happiness means that the ADHD person feels safe and loved by you. We've spent a lifetime being told we're 'too much' and that we need to 'calm down'. This has caused us to hide our true self and pretend to be 'normal'.

What's the definition of true ADHD love? Here are a few suggestions:

- Being able to fully unmask in front of each other and show your true self without shame or judgement.

- Being able to sit in silence without awkwardness.

- Being able to do star jumps together without embarrassment.

- Being able to act on the impulse to go for a random midnight drive while listening to loud music without feeling odd because you both understand that sometimes you simply need to follow the dopamine.

'I've researched ADHD, I get why that happened'

When there is a deep understanding of the complexities of ADHD within a relationship there is a considerably higher chance of maintaining a loving connection.

When your partner shows a genuine curiosity in your brain and takes time to research ADHD (and when you research the complexities of their neurotype), you are intentionally displaying your love for each other. It's a clear sign that you deeply value the relationship and that you don't want to lose it. Only after researching ADHD would someone truly understand the damage that can be caused by telling an ADHD partner to 'calm down'. Even with the most innocent of intentions, this statement can bring back hard memories for the ADHD partner and cause an RSD flare-up. The loving bond between the partners is strengthened when each of you allows space for intense bursts of excitement without either of you feeling judged or shamed.

One day, my partner and I were watching TV. She turned to me and said, 'What do you fancy for dinner tonight?'

My mind went blank. I was frustrated because this question always overwhelms me. I instantly thought of the perfect solution. I said, 'Let's write our own cookbook! Let's drive to the hobby craft shop and buy the bits we need to make it.'

Without hesitation, we both jumped up from the sofa and left. We had a great time buying all the items and spent the evening crafting the most beautiful recipe book together. My ADHD craving to impulsively craft something was satisfied and we now had a cookbook containing all our favourite meals.

If there wasn't an understanding of ADHD between my partner and I, I wouldn't have felt safe to act on my impulses because I would have feared being judged or shamed. However, she has spent many hours researching ADHD and because of this we enjoy these spontaneous moments together. She's put in the time to understand my brain, and I have with hers, and that signals to both of us that we love each other.

Here's a gentle reminder

Most people know that we can have difficulty remembering stuff. We've been shamed for it our whole lives.

Having a romantic partner who can give you little nudges to remind you about appointments without making you feel shamed is the loveliest thing. It reminds us that they understand our brain and, more importantly, it shows how much they care for us because they are respectful of our sensitivity to criticism. It shows they don't want us to hurt.

'Hey Alex, just giving you a nudge about that thing later on' might sound patronizing or trivial to a neurotypical person, but to me, a forgetful ADHDer, it's a much-needed lifeline and a reminder of how much my partner cares about my wellbeing.

Creating an ADHD-friendly communication style

It's a good idea to set aside time every day or week to communicate with our partners in a meaningful way. For an ADHD person, 'meaningful' means absorbing what is being said and responding in a way that doesn't feel forced or contrived.

Communicate in a way that works for you. Some examples of what you can consider are listed here:

> I'm much better at meaningful conversations when my body is preoccupied with a task.

> I'm really good at communicating when I'm driving, jogging or cleaning.

> I'm terrible at communicating when I'm not moving. My mind searches for stimulation and focuses on everything apart from what my partner is saying.

By acknowledging that you feel more able to communicate in a certain way and recognizing that some scenarios are simply terrible for you, you can have more meaningful conversations with your partner and avoid the arguments that happen when they feel as though you're not listening.

Just existing together counts too

You can spend quality time with your partner without having to verbally communicate because speaking can be a lot to manage sometimes, especially after a particularly stressful day. Being able to coexist in the same space without feeling awkward is a sign of a deep connection between the two of you.

You could be reading a book while your partner is doing a puzzle. Or you could be playing computer games together in silence. Parallel play enables you to share each other's energy without feeling the pressure to have a conversation.

You can create a mutually understood word with your partner (e.g. zonked) that tells your partner you've had an overwhelming day and that you're excited for an evening together without any expectation of verbal communication.

Sometimes all we need is a silent hug.

I can't do it for myself, but I love doing it for you

I struggle to do certain things for myself, but I enjoy doing those same things for the person I love.

I understand how challenging emptying the washing machine is, but I find it easier when I know doing it will make my partner's life easier. The thought of making my partner happy fills me with motivation to do the thing that I know they need doing.

I noticed you were struggling with that thing, so I bought you this to help

I've already mentioned the whiteboard my partner bought me when she realized I was becoming overwhelmed with the podcast admin. It sits on my desk and is a daily reminder of her willingness to understand ADHD. I thought that was lovely, but it was what she did next that blew me away.

Let me set the scene: I travel to London a lot to record the podcast. I take my laptop in a backpack. My phone travels in my hand. However, without fail, I always forget to pack my phone charger. My phone's battery runs out halfway through the day, which causes me difficulties because my train ticket is stored in it.

My partner noticed my struggles and immediately bought me a backpack with a power bank and phone charger built into it. She recognized that my executive functioning challenges were not going to allow me to solve this problem myself. I was too busy hyper-focusing on the podcast.

The solutions don't always have to be physical objects. They can be acts of service. For example, when you go out to a restaurant, your partner might recognize that you're feeling anxious and order for you. Or you might be overwhelmed with the menu so your partner can remind you of meals you have enjoyed in the past.

I have a partner who adores me for my strengths but also creates solutions for my challenges and for that I feel incredibly lucky. Buying or creating innovative solutions for your partner's challenges is a beautiful way to demonstrate your love for them. 'I researched your problem. Here are some solutions' translates into 'I love you' for an ADHD person.

Accepting the same song will be on repeat for a road trip

In past relationships, I've felt shamed for acting in certain ways. For example:

- I would eat the same meal for days until I got bored of it.

- I would listen to a song on repeat.

- I would impulsively start a new hobby but then get bored of it the next day.

- I would be called 'rude' for interrupting mid-sentence when all I was trying to do was share a relatable story to make them feel less alone.

In my current relationship, the shame has been replaced with acceptance. The bond between us is stronger because we both feel that we can act in accordance with our true unmasked self without feeling embarrassed or weird. We embrace the fact that the postman might deliver a package and one of us looks at it and says, 'What's this?' and the other says, 'I bought you a thing about your favourite thing.'

We adore the fact that when we don't have the mental energy to verbally communicate, we can send each other social media videos instead.

We never tell each other that we're 'too loud' or that we need to 'calm down'. We don't shame each other for big emotions. We give each other hydration check-ups. We try really hard to not interrupt when the other is speaking even though we have a million side thoughts to share. We remind each other to move the car so we don't get the fifth parking ticket this month.

Ultimately, an ADHD relationship flourishes when there is understanding, acceptance and a complete removal of shame. That's the key. It all starts with awareness.

'I looked for information about ADHD' is the most loving sentence we can hear. It makes us feel seen. It makes us feel heard. It makes us feel safe. It makes us feel loved. We've masked for so long because we've been taught that everything about us is 'too much'. We're scared of being vulnerable because we've been hurt badly in the past.

We're fragile in the face of rejection, but that fragility is also what makes us fiercely loyal.

We might get mad sometimes, but that's not a reflection of how we feel about you, so please don't make it change how you feel about us.

We'll zone out in conversations, but that busy mind is what makes us fun and exciting.

Our relationship will never be boring. Two days will never be the same.

I will love you like you have never been loved before

We want to be your everything and for you to be ours.

We will meticulously plan your birthday to include a meal in your favourite restaurant (although we might get the date wrong!). We will ask you questions, info dump with you, give you deep hugs, give you gifts related to your special interests, body double with you and research things you like. And we will forget you exist sometimes.

Thanks for understanding us. It means the world.

P.S. Saying 'I love you' feels awkward, but 'Here's everything I just learnt about killer whales' is absolutely perfect.

6

Dodging the ADHD tax

I've calculated my ADHD for the week and it comes to £275. That includes:

- the food that I bought but then forgot to eat

- that online sewing course I impulsively purchased on Monday but had lost interest in by Tuesday

- the extra electricity cost of having to wash clothes multiple times because I forgot to empty the washing machine again

- a payment of £19.99 for an app because I forgot to cancel the free trial

- all the vitamin pills I bought on Wednesday and the £50 gym joining fee when I decided to start my health kick that lasted two days

- the parking fine that I forgot to pay and which had therefore doubled

- a new phone screen because I dropped my phone

- a 2kg box of paraffin wax I bought from Hobbycraft when I thought my new calling in life was to be a master candle maker

- a trumpet (I'm still not sure why I bought a trumpet)

- buying a rug because my dog went to the toilet on the original and the thought of cleaning it was too overwhelming

- buying new socks because all my socks were dirty

- the petrol I used when driving to the shop to buy new socks.

I was going to calculate my ADHD tax for the whole year, but I lost interest before I could finish.

I once bought theatre tickets six months before a show. I didn't set myself any reminders, so obviously I forgot about it and didn't go.

I really want to create a service where people with ADHD could swap their hobbies for a few weeks, so they don't have to buy new stuff. It sounds like a great business idea that I'll forget to finish. My domain cemetery is big enough without adding www.ADHDHobbySwap.com to it.

Every time money comes into my account, I say to myself, 'Don't spend it all on rubbish you don't need. You need to chip away at your debt.' But the truth is, chipping away at the pile of debt doesn't give me any dopamine. I'd much rather buy that shiny candleholder or sign up for another online course to further my understanding of *insert latest hyper-obsession here*. Not to mention all the things we rebuy because we've lost the original one (or forgotten we own it). Can I interest anyone in some vitamin D supplements? I have seven bottles.

Let's face it. We're great for the economy.

I remember my first encounter with the dreaded ADHD tax. I was 18 years old. I walked past a car showroom. There was a brand-new blue convertible in the window. Without hesitation I walked into the showroom and spoke to one of the salespeople. He told me I needed a deposit of £1,000 to set up a finance agreement into which I would have to pay £350 a month for three years. I said, 'I'll be back tomorrow.'

I walked into the nearest shop I could find and signed up for a store credit card with a credit limit of £1,500. I was furious when I was told I had to wait three days for my card to arrive in the post. Three days later, I marched into the car dealership and used my new credit card to pay the deposit on the finance agreement. The car salesman shook my hand and walked me over to my beautiful new car.

It was so easy! I felt euphoric as I drove away. I only had to pay £350 a month. How hard could that be? But I had a problem. I didn't have a job. And I needed to pay the £350 a month plus the insurance payments plus the credit card repayments. 'Not a problem,' I said to myself. 'I'll get a job.'

I quickly got a job in a nightclub working three nights a week. This didn't give me enough to cover my monthly payments, so I got another job working the lunch shift in a pub. Sorted! Although I now had another problem: the car no longer excited me. In fact, I was bored with it and I had to work 50 hours a week, in two jobs I hated, to pay for it.

I didn't know how to get out of this situation. The thought of selling a car was too overwhelming, so I buried my head in the sand for two months. I eventually drove the car back to the dealership and asked them to buy it back from me.

I was terrified. I felt so much shame and embarrassment as I walked back in. I was scared of confrontation, so I didn't negotiate when they offered me a price that was considerably less than I had paid for it. I lost £3,000 in three months.

But that wasn't the end of it. The debt collection letters began to arrive. I ignored them at first, but they continued and eventually there was a knock at the door. I opened it to find a man who asked to come inside and seize my belongings. Luckily, I was able to negotiate with him and get him to agree to a monthly payment plan. My TV was safe . . . for now.

Before my diagnosis I simply assumed I was bad with money. I assumed everybody impulsively spent hundreds of pounds on their new obsessions moments after discovering them. Additionally, it seems cancelling my debit cards every three months in order to avoid the impossible task of cancelling subscriptions wasn't a sustainable solution.

It was a huge relief when I discovered there was an underlying reason in my brain for this behaviour and that there were real strategies to manage it.

I wanted to learn how to manage my impulse spending, so I invited Tina Mathams onto the podcast. Tina is an accountant who has ADHD and she has a special interest in numbers and finance. She teaches people with ADHD how to manage their money in a way that works with their brain and not against it.

Tina's first suggestion was to try putting a time barrier in between the impulse and the purchase. We both laughed and agreed this was easier said than done, but she suggested some practical tips to help. When you're confronted with the compulsion to buy something, it can be helpful to call someone who you can talk to about your potential purchase. This could be a partner or a trusted friend. This gives you the opportunity to share your excitement with someone, but it also puts time between your excitement and you actually buying the thing. During this time, you might actually realize you don't want to buy the thing anymore.

Info dumping our excitement to our trusted person can give us lots of dopamine and distract us from buying the thing. Often, after a conversation about the thing, we have received all the dopamine we need and no longer feel compelled to actually buy the thing.

We both agreed that it's not possible to totally overcome impulse spending (and why should we?), but we can control how often we do it. For example, Tina suggested, if your circumstances allow, having a separate bank account that you use solely for your impulse spending and giving yourself a monthly budget to have fun with.

It's also useful to only keep a limited amount of money on your debit card, meaning you will need to manually transfer money from your main account into the account connected to your debit card. This will take a minute or two using your banking app. This minute or two can act as a breaker and put that pause between the impulse and the purchase.

When we give ourselves permission to impulse spend, we avoid the shame and guilt that often accompany the spending. This helps us avoid the spiral that can happen as a result of feeling guilty.

More stimulation = less impulse spending

I reflected on my history of impulse spending and I noticed something that fascinated me. There were lots of periods in my life when I did *not* impulse spend.

I wanted to explore the correlation between those moments, to help me understand why I didn't feel compelled to spend money. Here's a list of times when I didn't feel compelled to spend money:

- When I was on holiday.

- On my birthday.

- When I met a new person.

All of the above situations provide me with loads of dopamine, so I don't feel the urge to hunt for it elsewhere. It hit me like a ton of bricks: I don't impulse spend because I need the thing, I impulse spend because I want to feel something.

We're not irresponsible. We're not completely reckless. We're bored. We don't need discipline, we need stimulation.

How to find stimulation

Finding stimulation is easier than you think.

- Have music playing while you're browsing the internet.

- Turn on the TV in the background.

- Play computer games.

- Call a friend.

- Go for a walk.

- Listen to a podcast while you're shopping.

- Use a fidget toy.

- Eat a sweet with a strong flavour.

All these things will help to keep your brain happy, engaged and stimulated enough to avoid the need to seek dopamine through an impulse purchase.

Distract yourself

I've adopted an unusual method to keep myself stimulated when I'm confronted with the compulsion to spend money: I hold my breath. I take a deep breath and walk away from the thing that's tempting me to spend money. This instantly forces me to focus on the act of holding my breath. I feel euphoric during the first 30 seconds but then begin to feel discomfort as I feel the urge to breathe. One minute passes and I'm sufficiently distracted from wanting to buy the thing.

We can also use our ADHD to our advantage. If you're in a shop and you see something shiny, you can tell yourself you'll come back next week and buy it. This is a great hack because it bypasses the part of our brain that's resistant to authority. You're not telling yourself you *can't* have the thing, you're telling yourself you *can* have the thing later. We'll walk away from the thing feeling like we have a plan to come back next week, but in reality we will forget about the thing and never come back.

The reusable shopping bag tax

I have a cupboard in my kitchen that's full to the brim with reusable plastic bags. I always get to the supermarket checkout and realize I've forgotten my bags and have to buy more. I've tried all sorts to counter this: I've put a sign on my door that says 'BAGS', worn a bracelet that says 'BAGS' and even considered getting a tattoo on my wrist that says 'BAGS'.

The sign and bracelet worked for a while until visitors took it down and I forgot to put it back up. The bracelet also worked for a while until I took it off and forgot to put it back on. I decided the tattoo idea was a little drastic.

One day, in a rage of frustration, I chucked a handful of bags onto the backseat of my car, drove to the supermarket and asked my phone sat nav to remember the location and to give me a reminder every time I arrived at this location. Genius! This worked well until the bags in the backseat ran out. My new problem was that I forgot to put new bags on the backseat so when my phone reminded me to grab a bag, I reached back to a seat of nothingness. Well, lots of rubbish, unused gift cards and expired coupons, but no bags. So I end up buying another reusable shopping bag for the food I've bought that I'll probably forget to eat – another ADHD tax.

Do it now (or our fines *will* double and we *will* cry)

Out of sight, out of mind (object permanence) doesn't just apply to things like friendships and car keys; it also applies to parking fines. How many times have we opened a parking fine and said to ourselves, 'I'll pay that later' and tossed it aside? Two weeks go by and the postman gives us another letter informing us the parking fine has not been paid and has therefore now doubled.

My personal record for a parking fine is £285. It would have been £35 if I'd paid it immediately. I'll be honest, I cried a little bit. When I get a fine now, I remind myself how much it cost me in the past when I decided to not pay it immediately. This is usually enough of a nudge to make me pay it straight away before I get distracted by something shiny.

But 'doing it now' isn't easy. Attempting to pay a parking fine feels like trying to stand up while wearing a backpack full of bricks. In these moments, we need to intentionally connect with not only the memory of what happened in the past when we avoided this situation (we know the fine doubled) but also how it made us feel.

I felt sad and shameful when my fine inflated from £35 to £285. I had to have a deeply uncomfortable conversation with my partner about it because we had made plans to spend that money. She understands ADHD, but that didn't make me feel any less embarrassed.

It's those memories that I intentionally connect with when I'm faced with a fine that needs to be paid immediately. The thought of reliving the embarrassment and shame creates an anxiety inside me that ignites the motivation required to pay the fine.

Some quick-fire tips the ADHD taxman doesn't want you to know

- Pay those tickets and bills immediately (we've already covered this one). If you can't pay it immediately, write it down on a whiteboard and hang the whiteboard in a location that you walk past every day. If you're anything like me, the fridge will work well. This can also be used to write down a list of the 'free trial periods' you have signed up for and will need to cancel.

- Ensure all your perishable food is at the front of your fridge and visible. This has really helped me to see what needs to be eaten and to avoid that expensive organic tomato I impulsively bought on my last health kick going mouldy at the back of the fridge.

- Sign up for a home-delivered meal service. There are lots of companies that will send you meals with the perfect amount of ingredients to make a delicious dinner. This also removes the overwhelm of having to think about what to eat. Plus, it's super exciting opening the boxes and discovering what's inside.

- Cancel free trials as soon as you've signed up (seriously, do it). When you see something in a shop window or online that you want to buy, set yourself a seven-day reminder on your phone. If you still want the thing in seven days, buy it.

- Put a little sticker on your car's petrol cap to remind yourself what fuel to put in. Having your car towed and removing the wrong fuel is expensive – trust me.

- Minimize late fees (and arguments!) by leaving things that need to be returned by your front door. Be careful not to trip over that casserole dish you borrowed from a friend eight months ago.

- Turn a trusted person into your accountability partner. Set up a WhatsApp group with them and use it to send each other reminders.

The ADHD tax isn't always avoidable, but we can reduce it by paying for it up front

Sometimes it's better to pay more for something for the sake of convenience than it is to pay less for something that you will not use. For example, I could spend £2 on a bag of five apples or I could spend £1 on a little packet containing a single pre-cut apple. By the time I get home from the supermarket, most likely the apples won't excite me anymore and they won't get eaten. But I can eat the smaller packet of pre-cut apples immediately.

The big bag of five apples that I won't eat has an ADHD tax of £2. The packet of pre-cut apples that I will eat has an ADHD tax of £1 (because it's cost me £1 more than the apple I would have eaten if I had bought the bigger bag).

Another example: I might spend 50p on a whole cauliflower, 50p on a whole broccoli and 50p on a bag of carrots. However, by the time I arrive home with my £1.50 supply of vegetables, I've lost the motivation and have no mental energy to wash, chop and cook them. I don't use them and ultimately they end up in the bin.

Alternatively, I could buy a packet of pre-chopped vegetables for £2.50. These only need to be boiled for several minutes and are much more likely to be eaten. The ADHD tax on the whole vegetables is £1.50 because they were all wasted, but the ADHD tax on the pre-cut vegetables is only £1 because that's the cost of convenience. The same applies when I buy small pots of Greek yoghurt. (If you know, you know.)

Other ways I pre-pay my ADHD tax include:

- buying a bleeping device that attaches to my keyring so I don't lose my keys

- getting multiple copies of my car keys made (for when I forget to change the bleeping device's battery)

- apps that help me keep track of my subscriptions

- using paper plates so the avoidance of washing up doesn't stop me from eating (I don't feel shame about this anymore)

- a few pairs of cheap glasses for when I lose/step on and break my nice ones

- bulk buying food and freezing it (this has been a life changer and it's so much cheaper)

- buying a dishwasher – the greatest thing I ever did

- treating myself to a home cleaning service during particularly stressful times

- having two dirty laundry baskets: one for whites and one for non-whites, because laundry is hard enough without having to separate everything

- vitamin pills that taste like sweets – they're more expensive but I'm more likely to take them

- spending more on clothes that have a longer return window

- bulk buying contraception because kids are expensive.

This logic didn't make sense to me immediately until I broke down the elements involved. The monetary cost of the item wasn't the only element to consider. I needed to assign a value to my energy.

As ADHDers, our energy is more limited and therefore more valuable than for neurotypicals. When I buy

something, I look at the cost of the item, but I also
consider the cost of my energy. Buying the pre-cut
apples had a higher financial cost but a much lower
energy cost. Buying the whole vegetables had a much
lower financial cost but a much higher energy cost.

It's so important to recognize that the cost of energy
fluctuates massively from day to day. On some days, I
might have loads of energy, so chopping up a cauliflower
has a smaller energy cost than on a day when I'm feeling
exceptionally drained.

I apply the following equation whenever I make a
purchase:

Financial cost + Energy cost = Total cost of purchase

There are some days when I'm feeling extremely
vulnerable and purchasing overpriced pre-cut apples is
actually cheaper because it has a lower total cost.

I was able to remove so much shame when I admitted
that my energy had a cost and that spending more
money in order to protect it was not a personal failure.

I'll buy ten things and return the ones I don't like

Let's be honest. This doesn't apply to us. We will buy
ten things, maybe like one of them and definitely forget
to return all of them. I can't even begin to think about
how much money I've lost because the returns window

has expired. Or I need to print out a label. Seriously, maintaining my life is hard enough without having to worry about how much ink I have in my printer.

Buying stuff is fun. Sending stuff back isn't. That pile of unwanted clothing in the corner looks like a mound of cement. It's impossibly heavy and I can't do it alone. So, how can we make it fun?

Invite a friend over (or simply have a friend on the phone) to act as your body double. You can even have monthly 'body double returns' sessions with a trusted person. You can also write reminders on your whiteboard (the one that's positioned somewhere that you walk past every day).

Similar to the shopping bag strategy, it's useful to store your returns in your car. This breaks down the task into manageable sections:

Step 1: Move parcel to car.

Step 2: Return parcel.

Returning packages is brutally difficult for us. For those of you that achieve it, I salute you. It's a *huge* accomplishment. For those of you that don't, you're not alone.

Invest in a good pipe cleaner

Let me explain: my kitchen sink gets blocked all the time. I don't have the executive function or the patience to wipe my plates properly, so I wash everything in the sink and let the grease pour down the plug.

My plumber used to visit twice a year. He told me to be more careful and not let liquid grease pour down the sink because it solidifies and causes a blockage. ADHD tax: £150 per visit.

I did some research and discovered I could buy a strong pipe cleaner (basically a chemical that breaks down the fat in the pipes) for £20. It takes 30 seconds to pour this down the kitchen sink every couple of months. I store the bottle in the same cupboard as my black bin liners (these are something I *need* to reach for frequently) so I don't forget it exists. I haven't called my plumber back since.

Creating a budget sounds like hell on earth but it saved me fortunes

Even uttering the word 'budget' sends a shiver down my spine. I'm terrible at organizing my money. The ADHD accountant, Tina Mathams, had some amazing ADHD-friendly advice on this. She highlighted how most of the traditional budgeting methods work well for neurotypical people but are very restrictive and therefore might be challenging for a lot of us. We need to budget in a way that isn't overly restrictive, otherwise our stubbornness and dislike of authority will make us rebel. This can trigger a feeling of failure that can cause us to feel shame – something we don't need any more of.

The solution? Instead of budgeting for every little thing, set yourself a few categories and budget for those. For example, you can set yourself a budget for eating out, groceries and new hobbies. This limits the budget to three categories and makes it much less restrictive and therefore more manageable and less overwhelming.

Tina also recommended keeping the budget 'fluid'. In other words, your budget doesn't have to stay the same every month. Our lives can change from month to month and what didn't feel restrictive last month could feel restrictive this month. This keeps us excited about the budget because it changes every few weeks. We can sit down each month and create a new spreadsheet. This will keep the spark alive and enable us to remain excited about the budget. (I never imagined seeing 'excited' and 'budget' in the same sentence.) Keeping things fresh, exciting and visual is important.

You can turn your budget into a game by giving yourself a reward when you stick to it. You can create colourful pie charts, stick them to your fridge and update them as you progress through the month. Should your circumstances permit, you could allocate a prize fund that you win if you spend less than your monthly budget.

I sometimes play a fun game called 'Let's see how many days I can go without spending any money'. (I don't count essential items in this game.) My record is 17 days, after which I buckled and bought a drill after I had a fantastic idea to stick a mirror onto my garden wall. That was three years ago and the mirror is still not attached to the garden wall – and the drill is still in its box. Oh, well.

The ADHD tax can't always be avoided but we can remove the shame associated with it and be kinder to ourselves (and even laugh) when we encounter it. Reminding yourself that it's not your fault goes a long way to removing the guilt and preventing a spiral.

Let's face it. ADHD is expensive. You can put systems in place to help lower that cost, but don't beat yourself up if they don't work all the time.

Be kind to yourself.

P.S. I'm off to buy some new houseplants because I forgot to water my old ones.

7

Preparing myself for parenting

My baby is everything to me. His beautiful face gives me dopamine every single day. I never thought I would love anything as much as I love my boy.

His wonderful existence in my life is the consequence of an impulsive act nearly five years ago. When my sister said to me, 'Alex, do you want to get a puppy?', of course I said, 'Yes!' I hyper-focused on everything there is to know about dogs. I went down the rabbit hole and came out the other side with an appointment booked to visit a litter of French bulldogs.

When I arrived, 12 adorable squeaking puppies ran towards me. Milo got to me first, so he came home with me. I was suddenly a parent – and one who was unknowingly living with ADHD. I struggled to manage my own schedule, diet and wellbeing and now I was responsible for someone else's.

There were definitely challenges at first – for example, keeping on track with his anti-flea medication – but I solved this problem by bulk buying it and setting myself reminders on my mobile phone. I even paid the vet extra for their 'text reminder' service. (Another example of paying the ADHD tax up front!)

I was so terrified of losing Milo that I bought him a state-of-the-art tracking device. It attached to his collar and an app on my phone displayed his exact location. But I never lost him because every time I walked him I obsessively focused on his safety.

I thought his little bark would be frustrating during a hyper-focus, but surprisingly it wasn't. He sits with me when I'm working, which I find really comforting. I also love getting outside with him because it forces me to exercise and that's so good for the ADHD brain. A lot of my best ideas have come to me when I'm walking Milo.

I impulsively bought loads of training toys but lacked the consistency to actually train him to do anything, so he still sleeps on the furniture.

Having a dog was a taster of the responsibilities of being a parent. I wanted to beef up my preparations for when I eventually became a dad to another human being, so I invited a number of ADHD parents onto the podcast to share the tips that parenthood has taught them. (Apparently, putting a tracking device on your baby isn't a good look.)

First up, I spoke to Geraldine Kostrewa. Geraldine has amassed a following of over 1 million people by creating content that helps other parents navigate parenthood as an adult with ADHD. She shared how her desire to do everything perfectly led to intense burnout, isolation and anxiety. She obsessed over parenting research because she wanted to get everything right, but it became too much and caused her to suffer severe mental health difficulties. She found herself neglecting her own needs and ultimately ended up in a really dark place. Her mental health took a nosedive and left her in a constant state of overwhelm and overstimulation.

This wasn't the first time I had heard about the crippling consequences of 'perfectionism', so I asked Geraldine what she did to overcome it. She told me she had embarked on a journey of therapy and intensive CBT (Cognitive Behavioural Therapy) and that the combination of these two had drastically changed her life in a positive way.

Geraldine said she had a lot of 'in-built' beliefs about herself as a result of early childhood messaging and that it was those messages that had created her perfectionism. The CBT sessions, as well as traditional therapy, allowed her to become aware of those internal beliefs and therefore let go of the guilt, shame and restrictions she had placed on herself, including her compulsive perfectionist tendencies.

I was fascinated to learn more about CBT therapy, so I was eager to ask Geraldine about her experience. She explained how CBT is designed to help make you change how you think about certain situations. Before CBT, one of her main concerns was her habit of ruminating over scenarios after they had occurred. (We ADHDers can often obsess over solving a problem, so when something doesn't go to plan, we obsess over what we could have done differently.) For example, if your child is unwell you might dwell on what you fed them and blame yourself for the illness. These obsessive thoughts can cause a lot of anxiety and guilt and even further your compulsion towards being a perfectionist; you're scared that it will happen again, so you obsess over feeding your child perfectly.

CBT can help to change how you look at this scenario. For example, instead of looking at it subjectively ('my baby is sick, therefore I must be a terrible parent'), it's better to look at it objectively ('my baby has never had food poisoning before, so this is an unusual event and not connected to my parenting capabilities'). In other words, remind yourself that this was an anomaly, a bit of bad luck, and it doesn't make you a bad parent. Of course, if your child is repeatedly unwell then objectively you may need to make some changes or at least contact your doctor to instigate some medical investigations.

Being a perfectionist might sound like an attractive quality, but in reality it can lead to obsessive behaviour that impacts our mental and physical health. Let's step away from the topic of parenting just for a moment to consider the role of perfectionism in the life of an ADHDer – understanding this could make all the difference to the way in which you handle being responsible for another being.

The first thing you'll need to do here is kick perfectionism in the butt: do the opposite of what feels right and monitor the results.

Many of us are emotionally damaged from years of feeling like we're not good enough. It's this feeling that instinctively drives us to do everything perfectly because we feel anything less will be met with a disapproving response. Disapproval is painful for us, so we'll go to exceptional lengths to avoid it.

The main way to make marginal improvements to our perfectionism is to intentionally be imperfect. For example:

- Don't re-read that piece of work before you hand it in.

- Delegate that piece of work to a colleague.

- Start a new project without meticulously planning every detail.

These three things go against our core beliefs that tell us we need to do everything perfectly. They will need to be done intentionally because you will feel a strong compulsion to push back on them and feed your inner perfectionist. But you need to ignore it, at least at first, and trust that everything will be okay.

Next, you need to monitor the results. Have a look at how you performed in that piece of work and how your new project progressed. You're probably thinking, 'I'm going to fail that piece of work, or this new project will be a disaster because I didn't re-read it or meticulously plan the launch', but I promise you the results will be nowhere near as bad as you think. In fact, the difference between the imperfect outcome and the perfect outcome will be minuscule. However, the difference in your mental health, energy levels and general wellbeing will be vast.

You'll also now be equipped with the evidence you need to convince your subconscious that being a perfectionist is counterproductive. It's counterproductive because being a perfectionist has a massive cost: its costs you your mental and physical health. It leaves you feeling anxious, overwhelmed and over-stimulated. And what reward do you get for spending that extra energy? Almost none.

Over time, your evidence of this fact will build up and the messages imbedded in your subconscious will begin to change.

Preparing for the ultimate responsibility

The thought of being responsible for a baby scares me. I frequently forget to empty my washing machine, so how am I supposed to care for another human being?

What if the screaming is too much? What if I get too overwhelmed and can't keep up with my parenting responsibilities? Luckily, after speaking to many parents, I discovered that this is a common worry and that there's a solution.

Step 1 (arguably the most important step): I will have to make sure my ADHD is well managed. Should I ever actually have a human baby to care for, the scaffolding I have around me to keep my ADHD stable would be in danger of becoming wobbly. So I would have to add reinforcements. And that means I will have to make adjustments in order for me to remain by my baby's side. Instead of jogging outside, I could exercise in the flat with the help of a YouTube video. Instead of meditating during my self-awareness exercises in the morning, I could meditate during the unpredictable moments of silence throughout the day.

Step 2: Being unapologetic in our efforts to remove shame. Here's the thing: I know ADHD enables me to do amazing things and I know it also holds me back in some areas. Parenting will force me into those areas where I struggle, i.e. organization, meal planning and consistency. I have to remind myself that my struggles are not a result of choice. They exist because my brain works in a different way from how society expects it to. It's not my fault and therefore I need to be more patient with myself. I *will* lose my temper from time to time and I will make mistakes, but that's okay because my intention is to be the best parent I can be and that means I'm not doing a bad job.

Step 3: Being aware of your cognitive load filling up. I invited Kirsti Hadley onto the podcast to share her ADHD parenting tips. Kirsti is the co-author of *The Journey into S.E.N.D. Motherhood.*[1] She told me about a brilliant analogy. She said it's useful to imagine that all humans have a cognitive load consisting of five slots. In other words, we all have five spaces in our brains. When we encounter something that puts a demand on us, one of the slots gets filled.

A neurotypical parent's slots will fill up with demands such as:

- I need to change my baby's nappy.

- I need to prepare my baby's food.

- I need to give my baby some medication.

- I need to buy my baby new shoes.

- Let's plan a nice weekend trip away with my baby.

However, a neurodivergent parent's slots will fill up with demands or questions such as:

- My baby's screams are over-stimulating me.

- I need to remember the travel directions to the nursery.

- Where did I put my car keys?

- What will the other parents think of me?

- I haven't drunk any water today.

Our slots get filled up much quicker because a lot of the demands that come with parenting are high 'executive function' demands.

How to protect your slots

The early stages of parenting are going to put a lot of extra demand on our brains so it's vital we protect our slots. Here are three things you can do:

1 If it's not a 'hell yeah', it's a 'no'. Lots of people will want to see you and the new baby so make sure you prioritize the social encounters that matter to you and decline the ones that don't.

2 Remove social media from your morning. Many of us wake up and immediately check our social media accounts. You wouldn't let thousands of people into your bedroom first thing in the morning, so don't let thousands of people into your mind. Don't let 'comparison' fill up your slots.

3 Ask for help. The moment you ask for help is the moment you increase your available slots from five to ten.

Here's some suggestions for how you can ask for help:

- Call a family member or a friend. They can help you with the bits you're struggling with, babysit your child or simply body double with you. Don't feel guilty about passing the burden on to someone else. Taking a break from the pressures of parenthood is vital in order to avoid burnout. Looking after yourself is an absolute necessity if you're going to look after a baby.

- If you can afford it, hire a cleaner. This is another example of paying the ADHD tax up front.

- Find your community. Whether this be on social media or through local support groups, they will act as a reminder that your difficulties are the result of a difference in brain wiring and not a reflection of your parenting capabilities.

The word 'routine' sends a shiver down my spine, but it's important to try to establish a structure that works for you. Use any quiet time in the evenings to plan the next day. What will your child be wearing? What will they be eating? Where will they need to go?

Our brain comes alive as the day progresses. Take advantage of your 'evening' brain by using it to plan the morning activities. Your 'morning' brain will be grateful. There will also be fewer demands on you in the evening as the world is winding down, so there's less chance of you being interrupted by phone calls, external noise and the postman.

Keep a pen and paper everywhere

Imagine the scene: you're playing with your child as your mobile phone rings. It's the hospital inviting you to book an appointment for your child's vaccinations. You agree a date and a time and end the phone call. It's in these moments that we need access to a pen and a piece of paper.

Invest in a clipboard, paper and a childproof pen for every room in your house. Find a high spot on the wall, out of reach of your child, and hang it on a screw. This simple adjustment will save you a lot of missed appointments.

Set a reminder to bond with your child

It sounds awful that we need a reminder, but in reality we can forget to maintain the important things in our lives. Schedule a time when it's just you and your child and really commit to growing that relationship.

I wanted to understand how we could best use these moments to build a deeper bond with our children, so I invited Jannine Perryman onto the podcast. Jannine is the founder of ADHD WISE and CEO of Neurodiversity Networks CIC. She shared the heartwarming story of how she formed a bond with her child.

She went into a shop and bought a soft toy; it was a cuddly little dog. She went home, sat on her son's bed and said, 'This is for you. His name is No Matter What. I want you to know that no matter what happens, I will be in your corner.'

Jannine explained how important it is to let your children know that you've got their back, no matter what, and that you're on the same team. I was struck by how simple yet how effective a visual representation of a parent's love could be, especially because I can struggle with verbalizing my emotions.

Next up, I invited Lottie Drynan onto the podcast. Lottie regularly shares her parenting advice with her 500,000 social media followers. I asked her a very simple question: 'Do you have any tips for a parent who has ADHD?'

Without a pause, she said this: 'You need to find a little pocket of time where you can simply sit in total silence, even if it's doom scrolling social media, where no one is talking to you or disturbing you.' She shared how lucky she is in the fact that her husband can look after their daughter, even if it's only for five minutes, and how this gives her time to sit in silence and decompress before starting her day.

I reflected on Lottie's great advice and began to think about how I would find those pockets of solitude. I created the anagram WEBS to help me remember the four parts:

W: Walk (go for a walk).

E: Early morning routine (create a morning routine that includes solitude).

B: Baths (have a hot bath in the evening).

S: Stretch (incorporate stretching in your day when possible).

Every part of WEBS can be as big or as little as your time allows. We don't need to get bogged down with the idea of going on long walks or creating a perfect morning routine. A walk could be as simply as pacing the length of your kitchen a couple of times. An early morning routine could be as simple as avoiding social media or intentionally having a large glass of water before you have a coffee. A bath could be every other evening if the extra hot water bill becomes unmanageable (although I advise allowing this to be one of those ADHD taxes we pay up front). A stretch could simply involve making the movement of picking something up from the floor more intentional.

It's the intention that really matters in every part of WEBS and that is to create a moment, no matter how small, where you can focus on nothing but the moment, and relax. These little moments are really important because they provide a pause between the demands of parenthood and therefore help to minimize the feelings of overwhelm.

Ignore the shame game

Lottie explained another fantastic way to create that moment of peace. She uses the TV or a device with a screen to keep her daughter preoccupied at controlled periods throughout the day.

There's a lot of shame surrounding the topic, especially on social media, where parents criticize the use of screens, but it's especially important for neurodivergent parents to ignore this narrative and not feel guilty for using a TV or a screen to keep their child entertained.

Back when we lived in tribes in small villages, parents had help looking after their children. These days, a lot of parents are left alone to do the job, so we should never feel guilty about using modern technology to help us create our own village. Having a moment to recharge your cognitive batteries will be beneficial to you, your mental health and your child. If it works for you then it's not a bad thing.

I was also very aware of the likelihood of having ADHD children, so I wanted to learn some tips to help prepare myself. First, I wanted to ask a professional how I could recognize ADHD in children, so I invited Sarah Templeton onto the podcast. Sarah is an ADHD author, an ADHD therapist and a counsellor.

Sarah told me a four-year-old child with combined ADHD (presenting with characteristics of both hyperactive and inattentive symptoms) might often talk a lot and move from one thing to the next. However, an inattentive ADHD child, who has a hard time paying attention but doesn't show any hyperactive behaviour, will often be silent but always moving. I thought about my own horrible experience in the classroom when I was younger and I asked Sarah what you should *not* say to a child with ADHD. She explained beautifully how ADHD children have as much right to be their authentic self as anybody else and that means they might fidget, move around and get lost on their way to places, and that *none* of that behaviour needs telling off.

The worst thing you can do to an ADHD kid is to try to turn them into a neurotypical kid or bring them closer to a neurotypical one. Parents need to stop trying to knock the ADHD out of their child. We must accept it, without shame, and work with it.

Here's how to work with it:

1 Encourage physical play time and exercise. This will allow your child to have a release for any pent-up hyperactivity and also give them the dopamine they need to be happy. Use their hyperactivity to their advantage. Don't tell them off for it. Examples of physical play time can include running, playing 'hide and seek', going to the beach, playing with friends, ball games, swimming, skipping, dancing and many others.

2 Teach your child that hyper-fixating on a new hobby but then losing interest in it is okay. It's not a personal failure if they decide they no longer want to pursue a particular

interest. (Bonus tip: it's a good idea to buy second-hand 'new hobby' items or even borrow them from a friend or family member to save yourself money.)

3 Make 'effort' the metric for success. Starting a task can be extremely hard for ADHD children. They might not be able to communicate this, so it's important that they are encouraged and praised when they start a task and not just when a task is completed.

4 Body doubling is a great tool for kids, too. Cleaning their bedroom, brushing their teeth and doing their homework will be much easier for them if you are close by when they're doing it.

5 Connect with other parents and spend time with other ADHD children. This will help you to learn by sharing common experiences. It will also enable your child to spend time with other children who share similar traits. This will put them in an environment where they feel less pressure to mask because there will be less contrast between their authentic behaviour and the behaviour of the other children.

How to correct an ADHD kid's behaviour without triggering an RSD flare-up

Imagine the scene: you're in a restaurant with your ADHD child and, as they mess around and fidget, they inadvertently throw their food towards the couple sitting on the table next to you. What a nightmare.

Sarah explained that in this situation, she would correct this behaviour not by 'telling off' the child but by explaining the effect their actions are having on the other person. She would say something like, 'The lady next to us has a very pretty dress on and if you keep throwing your food it's going to get ruined.'

Giving a reason for your child to stop doing something, rather than simply demanding your child stop doing something, ensures that it doesn't come across as a criticism and it puts them in control and lowers the chances of a tantrum.

How to interact with an ADHD child's brain

Sarah summed this up perfectly.

Number 1: ask questions. Don't tell. For example, 'Would you like to have dinner now or wait until your TV programme is finished?' rather than 'Dinner is on the table.' ADHD children like to feel as though they're in the driving seat, so ask questions to make them feel that they are in charge.

Number 2: choices. For example, don't insist they do their maths homework first. Ask them if they would prefer to do their maths homework first or whether they would rather start with their science or another subject. Questions and choices always go down well with ADHD kids. Start there and you won't go far wrong.

I wanted to pick Sarah's brain one last time, so I asked her for some tips for managing events such as birthdays or Christmas when you have ADHD kids. Here's what she said:

1 Do plenty of physical activities.

2 Don't let them have all the presents in one sitting but stagger them throughout the day.

3 Hide some presents throughout the house to create a treasure hunt-style activity.

4 Don't force the kids to sit at the table. It's not worth ruining everyone else's dinner when the child gets bored and throws a tantrum because they want to go and play. Let them go and do what they want to do.

Finally, I wanted to learn more about keeping a neurodiverse family functional, so I invited Hester Grainger onto the podcast. Hester is the founder of Perfectly Autistic, has ADHD, is married to an ADHD and autistic man and has two children who are both ADHD and autistic. That's a lot of neurodiversity under one roof!

I asked Hester what the secret is to keeping it all functioning and she said it's important to not sweat the small stuff. She explained how, when she was younger, she was always taught to sit up straight, to not fidget and not to put her elbows on the table. Now, she lets all that go. For example, her son doesn't like to sit at the dinner table because the smells from the kitchen are too much and he doesn't like the texture of the dining room chairs. I related to this because I often find the light above dining room tables too bright and the sound of others chewing fills me with rage.

Not making everyone sit around a dinner table at mealtimes was such a brilliant example of 'not sweating the small stuff'. It might be nice for neurotypicals to be grouped together, but it can cause a lot of anxiety for many neurodiverse people. When we stop thinking the traditional way is the right way, we can begin to make simple accommodations within our households that will make for a happier environment.

I asked Hester, 'What would you tell a neurotypical who was struggling to understand a neurodiverse child whom they see as misbehaving?' She immediately replied with how sad it made her feel that the question had to be asked and followed by saying it amplifies how important it is to treat everyone with kindness.

There is usually a reason for behaviour and it should invite a curiosity from the parent and a willingness to understand the triggers that caused the behaviour. Hester explained how giving your child the wrong type of spoon might cause a meltdown, but it probably wasn't the spoon that caused it; the spoon was merely the catalyst after a series of triggering mini-events.

I asked Hester how you can correct a neurodiverse child's behaviour in a way that won't make them feel broken (or won't trigger an RSD flare-up) and she said it's important to wait until the meltdown has passed and then, after an hour or two, ask the child if they understand why that behaviour upset mummy.

Hester concluded by saying that you can't simply not tell a child off but it's about looking at it with kindness and understanding what the catalysts are. She also said it's important to recognize that there might not always be a catalyst; they might simply be having a bad day. Throw puberty and hormones into the mix and suddenly you've got a rollercoaster. Are the actions the result of ADHD and autism or is it simply a teenager experiencing puberty?

Approaching the situation with kindness and prioritizing communication with your child is key to understanding their needs.

When researching for this book, every parent who is raising a neurodiverse child, or is neurodiverse themselves, said a similar thing: it's better when we 'allow for ADHD' or we 'allow for autism'. Let events play out. The critical part is the communication that follows.

Analyse the event, locate the triggers and share your findings with each other, and when things do get too much, as they will sometimes, and you do shout at your child, accept that it's okay because it's no one's fault.

Living with a brain that's easily triggered and easily dysregulated isn't easy, but try to enjoy the journey with your child and look for the similarities between you rather than focusing on the differences.

There's no shame when things go wrong. It's part of who you and your children are. Together, choose curiosity over judgement; choose retrospective communication over confrontation. Choose kindness … and don't beat yourself up if your processes are different from what other parents are doing.

Everything in my life vastly improved when I stopped trying to be normal and I don't imagine parenting being any different.

P.S. I'll definitely be setting up a regular automatic delivery of nappies.

8

How to start a business when you have ADHD

It was no surprise to me that people with ADHD are far more likely to start a business; we are natural entrepreneurs. Our internal desire to create stuff combined with an attitude to risk that many others might try to subdue ('don't do that, it's too dangerous' comes to mind) makes us the perfect candidates to start companies. We're great at spotting trends, we're calm in a crisis and our out-of-the-box thinking enables us to see opportunities that others miss.

As mentioned earlier in the book, I had my first attempt at the entrepreneurial life at six years old when I designed a board game. Other kids my age were happy playing in the park, but I preferred to be creating stuff at home.

I started many 'companies' throughout my earlier years: a car washing business, a boot sale business, a comic book collection business. When I discovered the internet, at the age of 14, I created a website called Quick Presents that helped you choose a present for a loved one if you were struggling for ideas. For example, you could type your parents' interests into my website and my algorithm would use that information to generate gift suggestions. The revenue came from an affiliation with Amazon.

Next, in my first year of university, I spent half my student loan on a giant industrial freezer. It was as big as a small car. I filled it with frozen pizzas and when a student wanted a pizza after their night out, I would cook one and deliver it to whoever had ordered it. I had four students working for me, cycling around Oxford at silly times in the morning, delivering pizzas to hungry students. It was going great, until the local authorities shut me down because I didn't have a food safety hygiene certificate.

All my early companies had the same life cycle:

1 I had an idea.

2 I got very, very excited about that idea.

3 I spent time and/or money on the idea.

4 The idea was profitable for a while.

5 I lost interest in the idea.

Even with my pizza delivery company, I was relieved when the authorities shut me down because I knew my interest had faded. Being forced to quit gave me a 'way out' that avoided the feeling of shame when people asked me, 'Why did you quit?'

I remember experiencing a lot of shame in the times between my abandoned business attempts. I excitedly shared my ideas with everyone around me but then had no concrete answer when people asked for an update six months later.

I didn't know I was living with ADHD at the time; I honestly thought I was useless and a terrible businessman. Starting and then abandoning countless businesses left me feeling that I was destined to do something else. I had no idea about the classic 'boom and bust' cycle that is often associated with ADHD.

But the truth was, I was capable, I just wasn't identifying what the good business ideas were and what the bad business ideas were. I wasn't spending time separating the ideas that simply gave me a rush of excitement from the ideas that connected with my core motivations.

How to identify the good business ideas

Creating two companies on social media, a landscape that I love, made me aware of the importance of choosing to work on projects that connect with your core motivations. A good business idea is one that does exactly this.

Discovering what your core motivations are is a process that can be sped up by meditation, journalling and deep introspective work, but in the context of an ADHDer starting a business, I always recommend a process called The Idea Shelf.

The Idea Shelf is a metaphorical shelf that all new ideas sit on. If after two weeks you're still excited about that idea, you take it off the shelf and begin working on it. I know it's tempting to immediately buy that domain, but if you can hold off for two weeks, you'll find out if the idea truly connects with your core motivations and you'll save yourself huge amounts of time and money.

If you impulsively start a business, like so many of us do, without researching whether or not it connects with your core motivations, you'll quit when things inevitably get hard.

This is also referred to as your 'why'. You need a solid 'why' because this is the thing that will keep you motivated after the honeymoon phase of a new business has passed. For example, when I started my first podcast called *Walk Away Wiser* (the one where I impulsively turned my bedroom into a sound-proofed studio and spent a fortune on cameras but lost interest by the time the postman delivered them), I had a lot of excitement but I had no 'why'. I love business, but I wasn't in love with the idea of interviewing other business people. My lack of 'why' or core motivation meant I abandoned the podcast.

After my ADHD diagnosis, I fell in love with the idea of interviewing other ADHDers because I had a deep desire to learn about my own brain. I also felt a deep sense of injustice over the mostly negative coverage surrounding ADHD and I wanted to create a more balanced discussion around the topic. That was my 'why'.

Whenever things get tough or my motivation disappears (trust me, it does a lot), I reflect on my 'why'. I hyper-focus on it. I read my journals where I have documented it. I mentally zoom in on it and more often than not it's enough to get me over the procrastination hump, initiate a task and maintain my momentum.

Next, it's important to 'zoom out' on your business idea and look at it in its entirety. It's so easy for us to get very excited about the early stages of a business (and we shouldn't stop ourselves doing this – starting a company is fun) and not pay attention to the bits that come next. For example, creating a logo and buying a domain can be really exciting, but we need enough dopamine in the tank for what comes next: creating a marketing plan, doing a financial forecast, planning stock inventories, making a profit and loss chart, doing a competitor analysis, and so on. I'm bored just thinking about it all…

However, things get easier when:

- the overall business is a good business idea, thus it connects with our core motivations

- we have a plan to make a business that works with our ADHD brain and not against it.

Making a business that works with our ADHD brain involves a two-step process. First, we need to be honest with ourselves about what aspects of our business we thrive in and what areas we struggle in, and not be afraid to ask for help.

Delegating the hard bits, or the bits that don't align with our strengths, is crucial, otherwise we will burn out in our efforts to force a square peg into a round hole. In the early stages, where budget is tight, freelance platforms like Fiverr or Squarespace offer affordable opportunities to delegate. As you grow, you will want to hire people to do the bits that you find tough.

This might sound obvious, but I've witnessed too many ADHD founders try to do it all themselves and end up burning out and quitting because they are too overwhelmed.

It's common for ADHDers to feel uneasy about handing over responsibilities. For me, it came from a place of insecurity and a desire to prove I could do everything without help; it resulted in burnout, anxiety and low productivity. Handing over responsibility is extremely liberating; it's okay not to be perfect at everything and it's okay to admit you need help. No one has ever built a successful company on their own.

Second, we need to ensure our business never gets stagnant. I've started lots of companies in my lifetime – the ones that have worked, UNILAD, LADBible and now

ADHD Chatter, are built on a landscape that is ever-changing: social media.

Not a day passes without one of the main social media platforms making a tweak to its algorithm. To many, this would be frustrating, but for me it created a new mini-hyper-focus. This constant state of adjustment created the novelty that my brain required to stop it drifting off towards another activity. The podcast has the same effect because every episode I get to hyper-focus on a new guest.

How to stop your business from getting stagnant

1 Zoom out when things get boring

When things get boring, zoom out from the moment and remind yourself of your 'why'. Object permanence can make it difficult for us to stay connected with our reason for starting the business in the first place.

It's okay to acknowledge when the boredom hits, because it will, but we can distract ourselves in a way that's beneficial for the business. Reach for that notebook (or whiteboard) where you journalled your 'why', read it and enjoy the motivation that follows.

Take a break, zoom out, remind yourself of your 'why' and carry on. Your brain will thank you for it.

2 Treat your new skills as new 'mini-projects'

Your business will naturally adapt as it grows and you, as an entrepreneur, will acquire new skills and learnings along the way.

It's easy to imagine a new skill as simply a thing that's required in order for you to progress your business. However, this keeps our mindset on the whole business, which can be overwhelming and create a feeling of stagnation. It really helps to frame your new skills individually, to look at them as mini-side quests and to approach each of them with the same enthusiasm as a brand-new business.

For example, it would have been easy for me to put LADBible into a box and call it 'social media business'. However, in reality, it was a combination of the following side quests:

1 Learn about social media.

2 Learn about logo design.

3 Learn about copywriting.

4 Learn how to write an email to big companies.

5 Learn how to make a website.

6 Learn that I was terrible at maths and needed to hire an accountant!

As an ADHD entrepreneur, every business I've ever scaled has not been one continuous project but hundreds of mini-projects bolted together.

Side note: it's important to be intentional with which skills you decide to learn and which quests you go on – some will be necessary and some will be a distraction from your business. It's okay to deviate (follow that dopamine), but it's a good idea to do monthly check-ins to ensure your new skills are aligned with your business needs. It's so easy for us to go off on a tangent, to hyper-focus on a new hobby or skill, so it's a good idea to monitor what skills you're choosing to learn and observe whether they're helping you achieve your business goals or are pulling you away from them.

3 Create a new routine

ADHD burnout and boredom rarely come as a result of one specific thing, so it's important to keep all areas of our lives fresh and full of novelty. Your business might be keeping you engaged, but if your life outside work is becoming stagnant, the need for distraction will creep into the boardroom.

These changes don't need to be big. Change your alarm tone, switch up what you eat for breakfast, drive a different way to work, alternate between hot and cold showers, change your perfume, dance at random times – anything to pattern interrupt your central nervous system and keep you focused.

4 Gamify your way through the tough bits

I've always thrived when things are fun (or as fun as they can be), so I put systems within my businesses that enable me to connect with my inner desire for games.

I hate the phrase KPIs (key performance indicators) – it's too formal and sucks all the joy out of me – so I changed it to key present initiators. I reward myself with a present whenever I reach a milestone or achieve something that deserves some self-congratulation. For example, when LADBible reached 'X' number of followers, I secured 'Y' number of client deals in a month or the podcast reached 'Z' number of downloads per month, I would gift myself something: clothes, food or a little holiday.

I also used a point-scoring system and that really helped me overcome my struggles with task initiation. I allocated a score to certain activities and when I reached 100 points, I gave myself a reward. For example:

Reading an email: 2 points

Replying to an email: 5 points

Calling a client: 10 points

Writing an invoice: 25 points

I also graded each activity depending on how I felt at the time and adjusted the point allocation accordingly.

For example, my points would double if I was having an anxious moment, or my points would triple if I was having an anxious and overwhelming moment. Some days, I was too frazzled to do anything, so if I did manage to send an email on those days, I would automatically give myself maximum points and unlock the reward.

It's so important for ADHD entrepreneurs to recognize that our energy levels will fluctuate massively from day to day. What was easy yesterday might feel impossible tomorrow.

We might have been emotionally regulated this morning, but someone said something to us at lunch that has triggered an RSD flare-up. Suddenly we can't write that email that we were planning to send; we're full of intense emotions and because of this, we can't make that phone call we had in the diary so we need to reschedule it, triggering further anxiety because we now have to let someone down. We might have said 'yes' to a meeting last week when we were excited about it, but now the meeting is tomorrow, we're no longer excited about it; we're anxious and we won't sleep tonight.

Being aware of our fluctuations in mood and adjusting the points accordingly is critical if we are to properly value the game. Otherwise, our justice sensitivity will kick in, we will feel resentment towards the process, we will feel our actions aren't being valued and it will lose its effect.

Additionally, on the flip side, it's vital that we assign points to moments of relaxation and incentivize ourselves to take breaks. This might sound counterintuitive to business progression, but believe me, it's essential for ADHDers to take steps to mitigate anxiety and to manage burnout. The consequences of not doing this will be catastrophic for your business.

Here are some examples:

Breathing exercises between phone calls: 5 points

Taking a walk outside or up and down the office: 10 points

Sitting still in meditation for 10 minutes: 15 points

Journalling: 15 points

Reflecting on the previous social encounter: 15 points

Being aware when burnout is looming

It's common for ADHD entrepreneurs to overwork, stay up late into the night and push ourselves to the limit. We've spent our whole lives feeling we're not good enough, so it's no surprise we feel like we have something to prove.

We all need to be aware of our own early signs of burnout; this will enable us to take crucial steps to alter our path and to take the rest that we desperately need. For example, my early warning signs of burnout include:

- becoming easily agitated
- forgetting things I usually remember
- ordering takeaway food
- becoming less patient
- neglecting my self-care/hygiene routine
- shorter dog walks.

And my personal favourite: yanking my USB stick out of my computer. I normally right-click on the Desktop icon and click 'remove USB stick safely'. I know I'm entering dangerous territory when I stop doing this.

The early warning signs of burnout will be unique to each of us. You can identify yours by adopting a retrospective approach through journalling. I encourage everyone to journal their entrepreneurial journey. Whether it be daily, weekly or as often as you can, it should include details of that time period such as:

- your mood fluctuations
- how easily triggered by criticism you were
- how patient you were with boring activities
- the social interactions that left you feeling lighter when you walked away

- the social interactions that left you feeling heavier

- how often your mind deviated from your business goals

- whether you were excited to get out of bed or you felt you had to drag yourself

- how you neglected your loved ones.

A detailed journal detailing the above will be useful for us to read in the aftermath of a burnout, because burnout will happen and when it does, we can use our journal to retrospectively look into our state of mind in the lead-up to it. We can use this information to identify patterns of behaviour that indicate we are approaching a bad situation and with this we can make better choices in the future.

How to leave imposter syndrome in the rearview mirror

ADHD entrepreneurs often achieve amazing things, but we also often lose sight of the fact that we have achieved these things, which means we don't carry the self-confidence that achieving these things should create. Success amnesia (we literally forget about our success) creates a feeling of incompetence when we are required to do the same task again – we feel like an unqualified imposter.

I always use the ladder analogy when explaining my method of combatting imposter syndrome. We begin on the ground when we start a business and with every accomplishment, we climb up a rung on the ladder. If we don't intentionally celebrate every stage of elevation, we can find ourselves on rung number ten, looking down at the ground beneath us, and become overwhelmed by imposter syndrome because we can't remember how we got so high up. This can create an anxiety that stops (or slows) our progression when, in fact, we have risen this high through our own endeavours and we're more than capable of climbing even higher.

Every stage of the ladder climb must be journalled, meditated on and celebrated – we need to etch it into our subconscious and provide ourselves with reminders to fall back on when our self-confidence takes a wobble.

For example, when the *ADHD Chatter* podcast reached its first 1,000 social media followers, I wrote two pages in my journal, detailing my skills which contributed to that milestone and the time I spent working towards it. I reminded myself that I had achieved this milestone not by luck or chance but through my skill, determination and hard work. This exercise creates a powerful feeling of confidence that I reflect on whenever I'm presented with a similar task in the future. I also re-read my journal as often as I can to ensure the connection between its content and my subconscious remains strong.

We are all amazing. Sometimes we need reminding, and there's no shame in that.

Accountability is your best friend in the whole world. Seriously, I can't stress this enough. You know that feeling when you can't be bothered to clean your own flat, but when you're at a friend's house you'll happily blitz the place? Or if you've got someone coming over to your flat in 30 minutes, you'll miraculously spring into action and clean the place to a professional standard? Accountability is the driving force in both these examples and it applies to your business endeavours, too.

Here are some ways I create accountability for myself:

- I post about my goals on social media. This makes them public knowledge and because I don't want to let anyone down or look like I haven't achieved what I said I would, it creates a motivation within me that enables me to stay focused.

- I share my goals with people close to me – friends, family or my partner.

- I recruit an accountability buddy. This is someone I trust and who works with me to complete tasks. We also have regular check-ins to monitor each other's overall progress and to make sure neither of us has deviated too much from our goal.

When I'm having a particularly unmotivated day (they happen a lot) I ask my accountability buddy to call me, share a screen with me or simply be silent on the other end of the phone. We can feed off each other's energy and get stuff done.

Creating accountability in any of the above ways helps me to stay on track, stay focused and stay motivated. It has the same effect as body doubling, as in the other person doesn't necessarily have to actually do anything – the knowledge of them being present with me and aware of my goals is enough to create motivation.

We need accountability that creates real short-term consequences when we don't complete something. Too often, the consequences for not doing something are in the future and for the ADHD brain, this means it doesn't exist and therefore has no impact on our motivation towards doing the thing. When we ask our accountability buddy to create real short-term consequences – for example, we give them money and they keep it if we don't do what we said we would – it keeps the consequence of not doing the thing front and centre – it doesn't cease to exist, it remains in our mind and consequently motivates us to complete the task.

Here are some other examples of how you can use your accountability buddy effectively:

- Ask questions. When one of you starts to fall behind, the other person can ask them questions such as, 'Is there anything you need from me?' or 'When do you think you'll be able to finish the task?'

- Create a points board. You both start with 20 points. Every time one of you doesn't follow through on a task, deduct a point. Each time one of you reaches zero, that person buys the other a gift.

- Remind each other of the bigger picture. Talking about the 'why' will keep you both grounded and aligned with your core values.

Here's a list of the ten strongest things on planet earth:

1 Spider silk

2 Silicon carbide

3 Nano-Kevlar

4 Diamond

5 Boron nitride

6 Lonsdaleite

7 Metallic glass

8 Buckypaper

9 Graphene

10 An ADHD person's intuition!

Our heightened intuition is our biggest strength in business. We're great judges of character and that skill will protect us from being screwed over, but we need to be aware of it and we need to trust it. As I explained earlier in this book, I ignored my intuition when I started out in business and it sprung me into a five-year legal battle and nearly cost me my life.

We're great people readers so we can tell when someone is being genuine or not and we need genuine people in order to make our business a success. Every successful business on this planet is successful not solely because of the concept but because of the people within it.

Every ADHD entrepreneur should look at their business as a recruitment exercise. The business will only be as good as the people within it and your ADHD intuition will enable you to hire the best, most honest and most reliable people.

Your intuition is powerful. Trust it.

Do it your way

Throw the normal playbook in the bin. Most 'How to start a business' books will be written with the neurotypical brain in mind; the recommended tools and systems will be tailored towards a brain that's different from ours. We need to advocate for ourselves and that means putting systems in place that accommodate our neurodiversity. Here are some self-accommodations I use:

1 I use my email signature to manage response time expectations. This is a great space for people within your business, clients or suppliers to become aware

that your response times might be different from those they are used to. I write, 'Thank for your email. If it's not urgent, I will reply within 2–3 business days. Thank you for your patience.' This slows everything down and puts me in charge of the pace.

You don't need to give a rationale behind this email signature. The truth is, a lot of people with ADHD aren't always in 'reply mode', especially if the reply requires a lot of mental energy and planning. Our productivity bursts come at random times and there's no guarantee we will be experiencing one as we receive a new email. Read it, make sure it doesn't need an immediate reply and then park it for later.

2 Whiteboards, whiteboards and more whiteboards. I've spoken a lot in this book about object permanence and the fact that when something is out of mind, it ceases to exist. This is true for many things in our business: appointment times, our calendar, our 'to do' list, our goals, our financial budget and even those emails we said we would reply to in 2–3 business days.

The day I embraced having a whiteboard in every room of my home and office was the day I started to succeed in business.

3 Create your own encryption and write down your passwords. This goes against every bit of computer security advice out there, but it's saved me so much money and time.

Always write down your passwords, but only after
you've created an encryption code so no one will be
able to understand them. For example, every letter
you write down is actually two letters before the
actual letter in the alphabet. You can't go back two
spaces before the letters 'A' and 'B', so these two will
change to either '1' or '2'. So if my password was
'elephant', I would write down 'cjcnf1lr'.

It's much easier to remember a single encryption code
than it is to remember multiple different passwords;
just make sure you don't forget the code, and make
sure it's different from the one in this book. ADHD
entrepreneurs are brilliant in so many ways, but ask us
to remember a password and our empire can collapse.
Have fun making an encryption code. Don't tell
anyone what it is. Remember it. Win.

4 I allow myself time to hyper-focus on stuff that's
unrelated to the business. We can get a million ideas
a minute, so it's no surprise that a lot of them will be
unrelated to our business. It's important to be kind to
ourselves when we gravitate towards a hyper-focus
that's seemingly pulling us away from our business
goals. It's okay to spend an evening researching the
ancient Egyptians or the mating habits of polar bears;
our brain needs time to feed on new dopamine. It's
a healthy break that will give us the rest we need to
attack our business goals with a fresh head.

5 I embrace *not* having a plan. I've never sat down and planned out my businesses; I find this process overwhelming and it blocks me from starting anything. This is hard for a non-ADHD person to understand, but I simply 'do' and I trust my process enough to be confident in the fact that all my 'do's' will add up to something great.

Creating a business plan, a profit/loss chart and other business projections are widely considered a necessity, but I've always found them to be an unnecessary burden. I know how to create a great business, just please don't ask me to show my workings.

6 No meetings (unless absolutely necessary). Meetings make me anxious. If I know I have a meeting at 3 p.m., I won't be able to do anything before 3 p.m., I'll be in waiting mode. Therefore, I always ask myself, 'Could that meeting be an email instead?' Most of the time, the answer is yes. 'Could that meeting be an email instead?' will make any ADHD business more streamlined, more efficient and considerably less anxious.

7 Avoid the unnecessary. The energy of an ADHD entrepreneur is precious and must be protected at all costs. We will have lots of people and things that are hungry for our attention. When presented with an opportunity, we must always tell ourselves, If it's not a 'hell yes', it's a 'no'. We need to trust our gut and have confidence in our ability to answer this question.

Lots of ADHD entrepreneurs say 'yes' to too much, deplete their energy levels on things that aren't driving them towards their business goals, burn out and ultimately end up quitting. Remember: if it's not a 'hell yes', it's a 'no'.

8 Prioritize your personal development plan. It's very easy for us ADHDers to go full steam ahead towards our business goals, but we need to find time to maintain our PDP. For me, this has always looked like a pyramid with three levels. The bottom level, the widest one, is called 'Self-Awareness'. The middle level is called 'Action' and the top level is called 'Goals'. The bottom and top levels, our self-awareness and goals, always need to be aligned, while the action is what we need to do in order to achieve our goals.

Working on my self-awareness will keep me aware of my core values. If I don't work on my self-awareness, something within me might change without me knowing, my core values might change and they won't be aligned to my goals anymore. If this happens, there won't be any internal passion to motivate me when times get hard.

An entrepreneur who continues to work towards their goals after their core values have unknowingly changed is walking a path to almost certain failure. This is especially tricky for us ADHDers – our emotional dysregulation can cause a blur in the line between our core values and a short-term obsession. It's why so many of us start projects but fail to finish them.

I've spoken a lot in this book about building our self-awareness; all those tips apply here too, but I wanted to include some specific advice relating to self-awareness in the context of starting a business.

In order to work on your self-awareness, analyse your emotions during and after a professional social encounter. Did you feel anxious? Did you leave the meeting feeling drained? Were you triggered by anything that was said in the meeting? Did you feel you needed to mask? Did you leave the meeting feeling motivated to pursue your business goals or did you leave feeling deflated and wanting to quit? Write down the answers to these questions in a diary and reflect on them from time to time.

If you're continuously leaving meetings feeling negative emotions, it may be a sign that your pyramid's lower level, your self-awareness, has shifted from your goals. It doesn't necessarily mean that your business is on a path to failure; it probably just means you need to make some adjustments to your middle pyramid layer, your actions, in order to keep everything aligned. These actions could be as simple as:

- only scheduling meetings after midday because your brain isn't ready to socialize before noon

- only scheduling meetings before 2 p.m. because your brain is frazzled in the late afternoon

- taking more breaks

- turning the meeting into a walking meeting –
  movement is brilliant for the ADHD mind

- keeping your camera turned off during a virtual meeting

- avoiding meeting times that clash with the rush-hour
  commute.

Three-hundred-and-sixty-degree feedback: not for the faint-hearted

The fastest way to gather feedback on yourself is to do
something called three-hundred-and-sixty-degree feedback.
This is when you ask those around you – business partners,
colleagues and other business associates – to give you
anonymous feedback based on their interactions with you.

This can be done by emailing pre-written questionnaires
to them. The questions can look like this:

- What do you think my three biggest professional
  strengths are?

- What do you think I have done particularly well in
  the last six months?

- What problem do you think I've solved particularly
  well in the last six months?

- Can you describe a time when you thought I was
  particularly motivated?

- Can you describe a time you were impressed with my work?

Don't worry, it's not as bad for our RSD as you're thinking! A lot of us are extremely sensitive to criticism, but in my experience, when it's received anonymously, and in the context of only positive performances within my business, it doesn't sting so much because I can look at it objectively and choose whether or not I agree with it.

It's essential that the feedback comes with a detailed justification because when we're given a reason for the change, it makes it make sense.

Again, I must stress, I know this sounds like an RSD minefield, but in reality it's not that bad and it creates an alternative view of yourself.

I recommend doing this exercise every six months to maintain your three-hundred-and-sixty-degree perspective of yourself. I strongly believe the benefits of this exercise outweigh the negatives and I attribute it to a lot of my achievements, but please proceed with caution.

Know your brain like the back of your hand

It's important for all of us to be aware of our triggers and the situations we struggle in. For example, I'm not good at doing lots of things at the same time. Trust me, I've

tried, and I've ended up paralysed with 'task overload'.
When I approach a task now, I look at it from afar and
then break it apart into manageable bits. This obviously
makes it less overwhelming, but it also enables me to
assign a separate deadline to each mini-bit and I share
these deadlines with my accountability buddy. I also look
at each separate mini-bit and decide whether it's a task I
should do or if it's a task that should be delegated.

Building self-awareness can be scary, but that's okay.
There are three things that block people from working
on their self-awareness:

1 Fear. Humans are conditioned to look outside
   themselves to notice details in others. Especially for us
   ADHDers, it's easy to analyse other people's behaviour
   and become aware of other people's intentions. We're
   especially good at reading other people, but reading
   ourselves can be scary because we subconsciously
   already think that we're damaged; we're living
   with a lifetime of negative comments ingrained in
   our psyche, thousands of mini-criticisms that have
   compounded to create a deep feeling of inadequacy.

   We know what's inside us and it's easier to ignore it.
   But we need to remind ourselves that those criticisms,
   although very real, were the consequence of actions
   outside of our sphere of control; they weren't our
   fault. We were never broken, just different; the world
   never realized it, so we were given a hard time.

It's important to keep this realization at the front of our mind because it enables us to look within ourselves without fear, shame or judgement.

2 Bias. Lots of people don't work on their self-awareness because they are living with a bias. Maybe they feel they should act a certain way because that's how their family acts; maybe they should apply for a particular job because that's what their parents expect. There are lots of biases that might be dictating someone's path, consciously or unconsciously, so it's a good idea to check in on your actions from time to time to make sure they're aligned with your core values and not anyone else's.

3 Lack of awareness. Finally, lots of people simply don't recognize the need to work on their self-awareness. The rewards of working on it are rarely immediate and when they do come are difficult to measure.

This difficulty in connecting the work with the dopamine makes it hard to stay motivated. For example, if you want to get better at setting boundaries (vital for ADHD entrepreneurs), it's difficult to prove that any improvement is a direct result of the self-awareness exercises you did six months ago.

If you want to manage imposter syndrome better, it's difficult to prove that any improvement is the result of the 'mini-win celebrations' I described earlier, but just because we can't see it doesn't mean it's not happening.

It's critical that we trust the process. I've spoken to hundreds of successful ADHD entrepreneurs and they all have one thing in common: they prioritize their self-awareness exercises because they know this is the foundation on which their entire business is built.

Automate your way out of overwhelm

Automation is another key component in running a successful business when you have ADHD.

Set up those automated email replies, have landing pages where clients can easily submit their details, buy accounting tools that automatically calculate profit margins, streamline communication channels with your partners or suppliers, and set up AI-automated social media replies that will deal with a lot of client concerns without you having to think about it.

I highly recommend hiring someone who can look at your business and suggest areas that could be automated. It might be costly, but it's good to remember that your time is very valuable. Set yourself an hourly wage (it's higher than you think) and compare your rate to the rate of people who are great at the hard stuff. Trying to do the boring stuff will pull you away from what you're good at and cost your business money in the long run.

If you have ADHD, you need to work on your business and not in your business. We need to take a wide view of it and make big decisions, but ultimately it's a good idea not to get bogged down with trying to do everything.

If you're anything like me, you're very creative but allergic to writing invoices; you're intuitive but cry at the thought of replying to 50 emails. Once we understand our strengths, we need to find ways to automate (or delegate) our weaknesses. And please, please hire an accountant.

Our energy is precious and we need to allocate it as efficiently as possible.

Don't overstimulate yourself at the beginning

When you have ADHD and you're excited about a new business idea, it's tempting to try to make everything super high quality immediately. After all, you're ecstatic about your idea and you want everything within it to be the best it can be.

From my experience, this is the fastest way to lose interest in your business. You'll spend too much energy trying to be great at everything. For example, when I started my first podcast, I immediately wanted it to compete with the best podcasts in the world, so I bought the best equipment. I spent so much time obsessing over trying to be the best that I didn't realize I was out of my depth. I had zero podcast experience, yet I was starting the game on expert level.

Trying to be an expert when you're a novice is exhausting – it caused me to burn out and it ultimately caused me to abandon the podcast within a few weeks. My next podcast, *ADHD Chatter*, started in my office. I didn't buy the best equipment; I used my webcam. I started interviewing people in private and honing my interviewing skills.

I made mistakes, like any entrepreneur will, but I made them in a safe environment and at my own pace. I didn't become overstimulated. I didn't try to run before I could walk. I didn't abandon the podcast. Six months later, after a culmination of new learnings, I felt happy to scale up the podcast and move it into a studio. I was ready.

So many ADHD entrepreneurs try to run before they can walk. The initial excitement of a new business overpowers the need to gain the skills they need in order to create their desired business. They then find themselves in an overstimulating and unenjoyable situation which results in them abandoning the business.

It goes against what many ADHDers instinctively feel, but it's vital to slow down. You don't need to immediately create a mountain. It will overwhelm you and you'll quit.

Start small: keep it manageable and grow it from there.

Embrace your ability to improvise

I'm not saying you should make it up as you go, but you should lean into your ability to think on your feet and adapt quickly when circumstances change. After all, it's what makes many ADHDers great: we take risks and we're calm in stressful situations.

You don't need to prepare for every outcome. You have more knowledge in your mind than you think. Imposter syndrome will try to convince you that you're underprepared, but in reality you're probably already over-prepared. How many times have you been anxious about a meeting, talking on stage or taking a client call, but then the event happens and it goes perfectly? In fact, the other people around you are telling you how well you did.

It's very common for the little voice in our head to make us doubt ourselves. It's vital that we learn to trust the process – we are better than we think.

It's also important for ADHD entrepreneurs to batch work. It's hard for us to control when our energy will appear and for how long it will last, so it's helpful to isolate specific tasks within your business that happen regularly, for example writing newsletters or creating social media posts, and to create a lot of them during the moments of high energy and focus.

I remember one occasion when I had a six-hour hyper-focus during which I created five weeks of social media content in one sitting. I crashed on the sofa immediately afterwards, but it meant I didn't need to worry about content for over a month.

Being an ADHD entrepreneur means defying conventional wisdom because, the truth is, most of it was written for neurotypicals. Ultimately, it involves a lot of trial and error to find out what works for your unique brain, what areas you struggle with, and then figuring out bespoke solutions that make your life easier, and not holding any shame if those solutions contradict what society tells you that you should be doing.

We also need to recognize that it's an ongoing process of self-discovery and not be too hard on ourselves if we don't immediately crack the code. This very fact is what makes ADHD entrepreneurs so resilient: we need to work that extra bit harder because not only are we navigating the business world, we're also navigating our brains and figuring out how to operate in a world that's designed for a different type of brain.

Always judge yourself on your outcomes and not your processes. Your process might seem weird to a neurotypical audience, but it's your extraordinary way of operating that will separate your results from those that are more ordinary.

9

Romance that works with your ADHD, not against it

I wanted to better understand the role ADHD plays in romantic relationships, so I invited Karen Doherty on to the podcast. Karen is a fully qualified relationship therapist, with over 20 years' experience, who specializes in neurodiversity.

I was keen to know the difference between a hyper-obsession and real love. Often with ADHD relationships, Karen explained, the early stages are incredibly intense. The two people's lives merge and they lose their autonomy; they cling together and lose their ability to have an identity independently of each other – everything is related back to the relationship. It can be too intense to bear sometimes; people are very sure that they've found their soulmate and this person is what they've been looking for.

Whether love develops out of that or not is different for everyone. The passion and intensity at the beginning are a big part of these relationships, a big indicator that there is neurodiversity present. This early intensity, especially in ADHD relationships, can last quite a while. However, nobody can live in this state forever. Something will eventually break it. Sometimes, a loss of interest will be the thing that breaks it. Sometimes, however, it will be a third person that breaks it: a child.

What's the most common miscommunication between an ADHD person and their neurotypical partner? Dating someone with a different neurotype can sometimes feel like you're speaking different languages. Karen explained that the most important step couples can take is to recognize where the communication is going wrong. You need a basic awareness of each other's triggers, otherwise you're setting yourself up for a turbulent time.

Communication suffers when there is an emotional trigger, especially with a neurodivergent person. Something in a conversation will trigger an emotional response. The neurotypical partner might not have realized that the ADHD partner has been triggered or that they've said something that has 'hit hard' with the ADHD partner.

Once the neurodivergent partner is triggered, their executive function begins to malfunction and for them the conversation stops immediately. From that point, you've got two people having very separate conversations. The neurotypical person, who hasn't recognized the neurodivergent partner being triggered, continues with the conversation. However, the triggered neurodivergent partner is now ruminating and raging over the trigger. They are thrown into fight or flight mode and they don't hear anything else after that point. Their mind is stuck and fixated on the sentence that triggered them.

For example: a couple could be chatting about their favourite TV shows. The neurotypical partner might say, 'I've enjoyed most of what we've watched recently, however that show about the killer whales was my least favourite.' The neurodivergent partner might suddenly remember that the killer whale show was the one they suggested to watch and become instantly flared by this comment because they've taken it as a criticism.

Their mind will flash back to the memory of watching it and hyper-fixate on the idea that their choice of show was not well received. It will feel like a punch in the stomach and an attack on everything about them and their taste in TV shows. They will be so engulfed in the intensity of the reaction that they won't even hear their partner ask, 'What shows have you enjoyed?', so will reply in a way that doesn't meet the normal flow of the conversation, or they won't reply at all. This will cause the neurotypical partner to think they're not being listened to; they'll say something like, 'Did you hear what I just said?' or simply 'Hello?', which might flare the RSD further and cause a bigger trigger to occur.

This is an example of a classic communication issue.

It's important to have an awareness of when someone in the relationship is triggered and also to have a way of communicating when the trigger has occurred. This can be a simple hand signal, a verbal 'I need a minute', or a code word you can use when you're with other people, followed by removing yourself from the situation for a period of time.

I wasn't surprised to hear Karen say that nine times out of ten, among the couples that came to her for help, when they removed themselves from the situation following a trigger, the rage disappeared very quickly; it was transient and forgotten almost straight away. I related heavily to this because I'm always living in the moment; I struggle to dwell on the past. It's why I can't hold grudges and why I'm often accused of being too forgiving. I can react really badly in the moment, but I can also forget about it if I give myself time to regulate my emotions.

Lastly, Karen explained how important it is, once time has passed and the emotional regulation has returned, to have a detailed conversation with your partner about the event. What was it that triggered you? Was there a particular word or phrase? Was it a tone in their voice?

Over time, these conversations will build up an arsenal of bespoke knowledge about what your individual triggers are and how to avoid them in the future. It will really help couples, where RSD is present, to avoid serious escalations and to calm them down before they reach boiling point. After all, when the emotional dysregulation becomes really bad and an escalation does reach boiling point, someone can say something in that moment of rage that can be deeply hurtful for the partner on the receiving end and the person who said it will feel great guilt.

How do you, or your partner, get over the guilt after saying something nasty?

In an ideal world, all of us would be able to remove ourselves from the situation and not say something nasty to our partners. However, in reality, we sometimes might not be able to successfully manage our moment of emotional dysregulation and we might say something unkind. Our partner didn't deserve to hear the words that just came out of our mouth. In fact, we didn't even mean the words that just came out of our mouth. We were reacting to something that happened long ago and our partner was the unfortunate one who reminded us of a past event. However, it happened, we said it and we must manage the consequences.

First we can apologize and explain to our partner why we acted in that way and why we said what we did. Hopefully, they will have an understanding of RSD and that will go some way to healing from what was said.

Karen explained how it's helpful to focus on the fact that the feeling of guilt you're experiencing is a conflated sense of guilt. When we zoom out of ourselves, we are able to recognize that guilt for what it is: a consequence of acting in a way that was out of our control because we were reacting to something long ago that wasn't our fault and that we are neurodivergent, which means our response will be much more intense than that of an average person.

Karen and I agreed that the biggest challenge in neurodivergent relationships is the ability to communicate to a neurotypical what and how emotional dysregulation impacts our thinking, and that RSD is the most destructive type of dysregulation.

Should you talk about RSD in the early stages of a relationship?

You have a much greater chance of maintaining a relationship when there is open, honest and aware communication around the challenging topics from the start.

When your partner understands RSD and the debilitating (and disproportionate) effects it can have, they are far more likely to show empathy towards the situation and be tolerant to our behaviour. After all, we know it's not our fault, but it's also not our partner's fault – it's not fair for us to assume they will be fine with us raging at them or giving them the silent treatment without a logical explanation for our behaviour.

We want our partners to think, 'I understand why they acted like that, it's because that comment I unintentionally made has triggered them. They need a bit of time to regulate their emotions.' We don't want our partners to think, 'What a nasty thing to say, they're a horrible person.'

It's a two-way process in which you have to be understanding and accommodating of each other's characters, both the good bits and the challenging bits. There needs to be a desire to learn and to be aware of every part of your partner's neurotype.

If you're being open with a new partner and they are not willing to understand the challenging aspects of your ADHD, then they are not worthy of experiencing the amazing positives that also come with your personality. With great minds come great spontaneity, excitement and fun, but also great sensitivity. Your partner must embrace every part of you.

Nevertheless, you must never use your ADHD as an excuse to justify your actions. There is a real-world consequence of your actions that you need to be conscious of. Your partner, neurotypical or neurodiverse, has their own emotional nuances and you must do everything you can to protect your wellbeing and to create a relationship where there is mutual respect for each other's mental health.

Create a plan to maximize time for meaningful conversations with your partner so you can both stay updated on their state of wellbeing. As with some of the self-awareness exercises I have mentioned in this book, it's important to maintain an awareness of the health of your relationship and the components within it. Try to stage weekly check-ins where you sit together and ask each other some basic questions, such as:

- What happened this week that made you happy?

- What did I do this week that made you feel closer to me?

- Have you learnt anything new about your neurotype that you would like to share?

- Is there anything you need from me right now that I'm not giving you?

- What is your favourite thing about our relationship?

- Is there anything new you'd like us to try together?

- Have you been feeling anxious this week?

- How's your mental health today?

Lots of couples get caught in a state of comfortable flow and fail to recognize the early signs of a struggling partner. Creating a safe space for regular, open communication serves as a great tool to spot the points of difficulty and to address them in the moment rather than allowing them to build up silently over time.

How to take responsibility for your emotional triggers

I reflected a lot on my conversation with Karen. She said something about halfway through our chat that I wanted to highlight here: people in romantic relationships, ADHD or neurotypical, can spend years trying to identify and manage their traits, triggers and emotional responses, but eventually we have to take responsibility for them too.

I asked Karen how this can be achieved and she said, 'By owning them, understanding them, sharing them and communicating them with your partner. This is how we take out the potential damage that they can cause.'

The ADHD relationships that Karen sees as having the highest success rates are the ones where both partners want it to be successful – both want to work and learn and neither wants to leave.

What are the early signs of a failing ADHD relationship?

Living separate, parallel lives can be an early warning sign of trouble. Of course, people should have autonomy in their relationship, but look out for the gap between you getting bigger and bigger.

Karen explained how this can be the biggest issue in relationships where the ADHD partner, who might be more capable of keeping themselves busy, spends too much time doing isolated activities, such as working too much in their office, and this causes an unintentional gap to form in the relationship.

Another example might be when there's an event in the calendar that the neurotypical partner has been looking forward to but the neurodivergent partner, who was excited about the event, is now too overwhelmed to attend. This may cause conflict as it can often occur unpredictably and at the last minute and often can result in the neurotypical agreeing to not attend an event they were excited about or attending on their own.

It's important to recognize when such things happen and ensure you communicate together afterwards.

It's okay for a partner to attend on their own and it's okay for a partner to withdraw at the last minute because they're overwhelmed, but it must be followed up by the couple's desire to communicate between themselves. This will allow you to remain autonomous but also ensure the gap between you doesn't unintentionally widen.

How to stop arguing with your partner in 30 seconds

People with ADHD can have limited working memory, which means they can only keep a small amount of information in their head at one time. So, if your ADHD partner constantly interrupts you when you're speaking, it's not because they're rude, it's because they know they will forget the thing they want to say if they don't say it straight away. In their mind, it would be rude if they didn't interrupt you because if they let you speak for several minutes, by the time you've finished and it's their turn to speak, they will have forgotten most of what you said and that would appear as though they weren't listening.

Another little tip: instead of asking your ADHD partner to help you with something *now*, ask them to help you with something in ten minutes. This will allow your partner time to finish their current activity and make it sound more like a soft request, which will massively help with their demand avoidance. These are small changes, but they will lead to a big decrease in arguments.

Here are five things that might be causing problems in your ADHD relationship without you knowing:

1 Rejection sensitive dysphoria. I speak about the dreaded RSD a lot in this book and for good reason. It's the most common issue I encounter, not only in my own life but also when speaking to others in the community and on the podcast. Among the many strategies I've discussed, another thing you can do is to adopt an approach that's overly supportive of mini-achievements. People with ADHD can be sensitive to rejection, but we can also be incredibly receptive to praise – we love it! Don't just praise your partner

when they achieve something major, praise them after the little things, too.

2 Being unintentional in your displays of affection. A lot of us love to be loved, we need reassurance and reminders that you're not angry at us. Neurodiverse or neurotypical, it's a nice idea to create little moments of physical touch to make your partner feel safe. For example, a hand on the lap when watching a film or an intentional hug when you arrive home from work (I call it the 'big squeeze') are simple gestures but can go a long way to staving off the effects of RSD. It's also important to recognize that this tip might not be suitable for everyone because some people get overstimulated by touch.

3 Avoiding the micro check-ins. When we go for long periods of time without asking our partner simple questions like 'Is there anything I can help you with?', it can create an unintentional emotional distance between the two of you. Even if the questions get a generic response such as 'I'm okay today, thank you', it reminds your partner that you care and that you're not angry at them, which also helps to starve you of the initial stages of RSD.

4 Assuming your partner can instantly transition from one task to another. It's easy to assume that everyone can immediately stop working on something and begin a new task or chore. However, if your partner is hyper-focused on something, it will be hard for

them to suddenly stop working on that thing and instantly transition into something else, such as making a coffee or cleaning the flat. Assuming your partner can do this can often result in a mid-hyper-focus interruption rage.

5 Failing to give your partner time to decompress. A lot of people with ADHD spend so much energy masking, pretending to be something they're not, altering themselves to 'fit in', that by the time they arrive home from work, they're exhausted – they don't have any energy left and simply want to collapse onto the sofa. It's not personal, they're brain fatigued. It's important to recognize when this happens to your partner, or within yourself, and to have a code word in order to communicate your need to decompress. Otherwise, the more energized partner might mistake the burnt-out partner's lack of enthusiasm for their conversation as a rejection.

The impulsive argument and how to avoid it

We ADHDers can tolerate a lot of little things because, if we're honest, we don't care about the small stuff. If the flat is a bit messy, the car has a scratch on it or the weather isn't perfect, we move on. However, we have a very low tolerance for injustice. If our partner makes a comment about us that we perceive to be unfair, we can snap and impulsively say something in retaliation. This impulsive comment can then easily escalate into an argument. We also don't have a filter, which can further increase the chance of an escalation.

This can be very common in ADHD relationships where one person doesn't understand the nuances of their partner's neurotype. In our minds, it's unfair when our partner misunderstands our actions for something other than what they are. For example, we could be overstimulated and therefore unable to start a chore, or we could be having a bad reaction to caffeine and feeling particularly anxious. In these two scenarios, we might shut down and be able to focus on the uncomfortable feeling only and how to stop it boiling over into a full-blown anxiety attack.

During these moments, our partner might mistake our inattentiveness as rudeness and make a little comment such as, 'Did you hear what I said?' First, we will feel mad because the comment has interrupted our hyper-focus on our uncomfortable feeling, and second, we will hear the undertone of irritation in our partner's voice and assume they think we're being rude. This creates a feeling of injustice in us because we know that's not true. In this moment, we might impulsively say something that starts an argument.

The solution is simple: communication.

It's important to communicate with your partner, in the moment, when these shutdowns happen so they know what's happening and that any response from you is not coming from a regulated place. Again, you might develop some code words, or a physical signal, to identify the various forms of shutdowns.

It's also important to openly discuss the shutdown afterwards so that as a couple you build upon your understanding of each other's neurotype.

Finally, it's vital to acknowledge that you're human and you will impulsively start arguments from time to time – this is perfectly normal and doesn't need to be surrounded by shame. As long as this is followed by a conversation, an effort to understand the cause of the argument, you can use the experience as an opportunity to understand each other's behaviour and to grow as a couple.

Our lack of self-worth is not our friend: how to shut it down

It's not surprising that many of us have low self-worth. After all, we've spent our entire lives being told we're not good enough. This feeling of low self-worth is ingrained in our subconscious, it causes a part of us to self-sabotage our meaningful relationships because it doesn't think we deserve to have them. It tells us stuff like 'I don't know why they like me' and 'they will soon find out that I'm weird and leave me'.

When our subconscious doesn't think we're good enough for our partner, it will make us do things to damage the relationship. For example, we might ignore the part of our brain that knows what our partner just said was harmless. During this moment, we will intentionally forget about our techniques to manage RSD and instead explode into an unregulated rage monster.

We do this because our subconscious wants us to trigger an argument that will sabotage our relationship. These moments come during times of extreme emotional tiredness, when our conscious brain is not very active, and they cause huge amounts of damage to our relationships.

To shut down our subconscious desire to self-sabotage, it's vital that we're aware of it. By being aware, we can acknowledge it, recognize when it's active and ignore it. Once we're aware of it, we need to take steps to take away its power. This can be done by focusing on the evidence we have that contradicts it – and we have a lot of evidence.

We know so much about ADHD now that proves that those people in our past were wrong. However, it's difficult to change our subconscious, so it's important to compare it with our new understanding of ADHD.

Your subconscious thinks:

- you're not good enough

- you're broken

- you're lazy.

Your new understanding says:

- you're enough

- you're different

- you're overwhelmed.

When we feel our subconscious desire to self-sabotage kicking in, it's important to remind ourselves of this new understanding. Meditation and journalling can be helpful tools to empower our conscious mind to silence the subconscious. Breathing techniques can be useful in the moment. Using a physical reminder, such as an 'achievement list' on your phone or a photo album full of your accomplishments, can also be useful to silence your subconscious during moments of impending self-sabotage.

Don't look for fun outside your relationship, create it within

Lots of people with ADHD crave novelty. It's why we jump into new relationships but sometimes get bored after the honeymoon period. It's the same reason lots of us struggle to maintain jobs and hobbies.

For some, hopping from one relationship to another might be an ideal situation, but for many, it's good to know how to maintain the feeling of euphoria, or at least a sustainable level of joy, so you don't feel compelled to leave.

Some of us feel that dopamine leave us after spending lots of time with the same person, but rather than hunt for it elsewhere, it can be replaced with another chemical called oxytocin. Oxytocin is released when we form deep connections with people and has a similar sensation to dopamine. It's our body rewarding us for being vulnerable and bonding with another human being, but it takes work to maintain.

Common misunderstandings

The most frustrating thing about dating someone who doesn't understand ADHD is being constantly misunderstood. I hate it when people call me lazy.

Look, I get it, I know I might look lazy when I'm lying on the sofa, scrolling social media, but inside my head I'm in a constant state of overwhelm. I know I need to take the washing out of the machine, I know I need to hoover the floor, I know I need to text my friend back, I know I need to check the oil in my car, I know I need to eat . . .

I'm burnt out just thinking about all the little things I need to do. I end up overthinking, over-analysing, end up in decision paralysis and do nothing.

I know you think ADHD means I should be physically hyperactive, I should be able to do all these things, but my hyperactivity is internalized, it's in my mind and it causes me a huge amount of overwhelm and anxiety. So please don't call me lazy, this isn't a choice, and please, give me recognition when I hyper-focus and do a week's worth of stuff in an afternoon.

Three things to know if you're dating someone who has ADHD

One: your ADHD partner most likely has a heightened sense of intuition, which means they can sense when something isn't right or when you're annoyed at them. Due to a lifetime of feeling different, they are primed to recognize the tiniest changes in tone of voice and mood.

When the ADHD person senses one of these things, they will catastrophize over the worst-case scenario and spiral into an obsessive thought pattern. They will be convinced you hate them and are going to end the relationship.

To avoid these spirals, it's important to communicate the cause of any tensions as they arise because the ADHD person will know they are there and a simple understanding of what has caused them will save any unnecessary anxiety.

Two: your ADHD partner probably does stuff which falls outside the perimeters of what society considers normal. For example, we might jump out of bed at 2 a.m. and decide to paint the wall a different colour, we might get the 'zombies' (the act of exhibiting an extraordinary amount of energy in a short space of time because of a feeling of overwhelming joy) or we might change our mood suddenly because the person at the supermarket till cut in front of us and it flared our justice sensitivity.

It's important to approach all these behaviours with curiosity and not judgement because the ADHD person might not understand them either and it can be a fun journey of exploration to embark on together. Not to mention the fact that being 'normal' can be incredibly tedious and it's fun to embrace and bond over each other's differences.

Three: your ADHD partner might say something that appears to be completely random and has no connection to anything that's been said previously. This is because a lot of ADHDers internalize their hyperactivity and have huge amounts of emotional internal chatter. They will embark on a thought process in their mind and when they do finally say something, it will be because their excitement has boiled over and they need to take action.

For example, you might be silently watching a film together. Your ADHD partner might be looking at the TV, however their mind might be elsewhere – thinking about your next summer holiday, for example. They might suddenly say, 'I need to find my swimsuit' stand up and run towards the wardrobe. You'll be left on the sofa, looking confused.

Again, it's important to experience these events with curiosity and not judgement. Allowing your partner to feel safe enough to act in this way around you is a testament to the strength of your relationship – they feel comfortable enough to act in this way, to unmask around you, and that should be celebrated.

ADHD relationships are beautiful things, filled with spontaneity and excitement, but like any relationship, also awash with challenges. Take time together to understand where your unique strengths lie and what you need to do to manage the more challenging parts.

The ADHD mind is complex. Be curious. Avoid judgement. Be kind and give patience where patience is due.

The reason for that outburst might not be as clear as you think. The reason someone can't get off the sofa and help with the dishes on a particular day might not be as straightforward as it first appears. There might be something bigger at play which explains why they came home from work and didn't have the ability to communicate with you.

Whatever happens, good or bad, always take the time together to retrospectively analyse the event, communicate your findings with each other and use them to grow your mutual understanding of how the other's brain works.

The road might be bumpy sometimes, and perhaps more turbulent than a neurotypical relationship, but over time the bumps will be less noticeable, the highs will be more enjoyable and your bond will be strong enough to weather the ride.

That's how you keep a relationship healthy, by understanding and accepting each other for who you really are, masked or unmasked, regulated or dysregulated, thriving or burnt out, organized or chaotically messy, anxiously early or frantically late.

You are each other's centrepiece.

You are each other's travelling companion.

And what a journey it's going to be.

10

Advice for my younger self

Congratulations on making it this far through the book! If you're anything like me, I know how hard that must have been. My bookshelf is full of books I bought on impulse, then read the first chapter and never touched again.

I wanted to use the last chapter to reflect on all my ADHD learnings and to share the biggest realizations on my journey.

So many of us grew up hearing things like:

- You're just lazy.

- If only you'd apply yourself.

- Just go to bed earlier!

- You're not forgetting, you're choosing not to remember.

- You're so dramatic. Stop over-reacting.

- Just think! It's not that hard.

- You just need to try harder.

All these little comments compound over time to create a person who feels that they're not good enough. But the truth is that we're simply different and that all these comments were made when we were being held to a neurotypical standard – and that's not our fault.

I strongly believe that ADHD is something humans evolved to better survive. It's why, when there's an emergency, the only one who's not overwhelmed and frozen with fear but *is* able to think clearly and know what to do is the ADHD person.

If you go back in time to when humans lived in tribes, a person with ADHD would be a huge asset – their unique way of thinking would ensure the collective survival of the tribe. Their heightened intuition would spot an incoming threat. They would be super alert to predators, their out-of-the-box thinking would mean they would know where to look for food and resources, they would have an animal-like survival mode.

But in today's world, there's less opportunity for us to showcase our strengths.

A lot of the stuff we're good at is now automated. For example, we would be great hunters, but now we have supermarkets. We would be great fire makers, great navigators and great defenders if our tribe was under attack, but nowadays none of those skills is really required.

Now, we have to conform to society's version of normal. We have to sit in an office for eight hours a day, we have to complete tax returns, we have to hold a conversation with someone on a topic we're not interested in. The skills we have aren't designed for today's modern world so it's no surprise we struggle sometimes.

ADHD enables us to hyper-focus on a new passion but doesn't always give us enough long-term energy to follow it through. ADHD gives us amazing intuition – we see and feel everything. We're hyper-aware of everything around us, but this can make us anxious.

ADHD can enable us to meet a stranger, become best friends with them, but then a month later we forget they exist because they're not in our immediate line of sight.

ADHD can make us fall in love super quickly, we hyper-fixate on that person and they become our whole world, but then two years later we get bored, yet we stay in the relationship longer than we should because our extreme empathy doesn't want us to hurt them. We have a phobia about confrontation so we avoid the conversation, but then the guilt tears us up because we know we're wasting their time.

All these things make it sound as though we're lazy or bad people, but none of these things is a choice.

Common misconceptions

I used to think ADHD meant that someone was hyperactive, but it turns out all the studies on ADHD were done on boys. Women and girls with ADHD can present very differently.

Women have become so good at hiding their ADHD traits because society teaches them that's not how women *should* behave. Women are so good at masking they have even convinced their doctors that they're 'normal' and then they get misdiagnosed with anxiety, depression or PMS.

Too many women and girls are living in a constant state of overwhelm, have crippling low self-esteem, struggle to maintain relationships, are ultra-sensitive to rejection and they don't know why. They feel misunderstood – and this can have disastrous outcomes.

One thing I wish more people knew about ADHD is that it doesn't always mean you're physically hyperactive. I have ADHD and my hyperactivity is in my head. It sometimes feels like five highly caffeinated squirrels are all barrelling around in there and it's the main reason I didn't get diagnosed until I was 34.

I didn't display any of the obvious traits. I wasn't bouncing off the walls, I wasn't a nuisance to anyone, I didn't appear to be full of energy. My ADHD lived inside my head. I had the inside type, not the outside type. Not the type that's annoying to everyone else. No one sees the inside type, but I saw it and it caused me to have a constantly racing mind, uncontrollable internal thoughts, decision paralysis, all of which kept me in a constant state of overwhelm.

I can sit on the sofa and be unable to move because the thought of doing everything I need to do is simply too overwhelming. I can walk into a supermarket and walk out empty-handed because I've been unable to make a decision about what to buy. I can read an email 50 times and not absorb a single word of it because my brain is whizzing from one thought to another at a million miles per hour.

All the energy was in my head and it was exhausting. I was diagnosed with general anxiety disorder when I was 15 and put on anxiety medication. I became so good at masking that I convinced my doctor I was 'normal'. I even convinced myself.

I was diagnosed with ADHD two years ago and now I'm wondering who I really am. What's me and what's masking? What's me and what's a coping mechanism? It's a fascinating journey of self-discovery that I'm going on and writing this book is making it a lot easier.

So thank you for the support, thank you for listening to the podcast, and here's a shout-out to all the late-diagnosed ADHDers.

Everything in your past makes sense. You were always enough.

Ignoring the haters

I didn't want to write a section of my book covering this, but I recently received this message: 'Mate, stop talking about ADHD so much. Nobody cares!'

To the person who sent this message, I have a message of my own for you. Here's the story, which I first told in the introduction to this book, of why I post about ADHD so much.

When I was a little boy, I was sitting at the back of a classroom when the teacher pointed at me and asked, 'Alex, do you know the answer to this question?' At that moment, my palms went sweaty, my face went red and my heart rate increased. In a panic, I stood up and left the classroom. I found someone in the corridor and told them to call an ambulance, I was having a heart attack.

Of course I wasn't having a heart attack, I was having a panic attack . . . because of undiagnosed ADHD.

I wish I could go back in time with the knowledge of ADHD I have now, put my arms around the younger version of me and say, 'You're not broken, you don't need to be fixed', but of course I can't do that. So the second best thing I can do is make content about ADHD in the hope that someone else, a younger version of me, sees it and it gives them the awareness which saves them from going through a similar situation.

I genuinely think my ADHD content is creating meaningful conversations and helping, albeit in a small way, to provide value to a massively under-served community. And why do I think that? Because I also receive lots of message like this: 'Alex, thank you for saving my life.'

And that's why I talk about ADHD so much.

Another message I often receive is this: 'You must be brave to talk about ADHD.'

I hear it all the time. And I always say the same thing: the reason people think it takes bravery to talk about something is the very reason for speaking about it. Because the presumption of bravery is proof that stigma still exists. And stigma is the main reason people suffer in silence and don't ask for help.

So, I'll keep talking about ADHD until I hear less of 'you must be brave'. That's when I'll know the stigma is beginning to disappear. That's when I'll know more people are asking for help.

As my self-awareness grows, I realize the importance of finding humour in the more challenging aspects of ADHD. For example, I'm *really* good at solving problems, but please don't ask me to 'show my workings'. I have no idea how I worked it out.

And there are more of such examples:

- Finally doing a task that I've been putting off for three months and realizing it took three minutes.

- Spending all day struggling with focus but then suddenly thinking of an amazing business idea and buying all the domains while deep cleaning my flat.

- Getting really excited about a new project (at 1 a.m.), jumping out of bed, doing the research, hyper-focusing, buying all the gear, losing interest in a week.

- Going on to Google, forgetting what I wanted to search for, checking my recent apps to see what triggered the thought, getting distracted by apps, forgetting about Google.

I used to hold so much shame over these behaviours, and sometimes I still do, but I'm able to look at them now with an ADHD lens, which helps me to add some important context: these behaviours aren't harming anyone and they're not my fault.

I find some things that others find easy challenging, but I'm also able to do a lot of things with ease that most people find challenging. I might not be able to immediately remember your name, but I'll be able to tell if you're a nice person or not. I might not be able to complete my tax return on time, but I can create the business that requires it to be done.

The key to ADHD management is figuring out where your strengths lie, being honest about what your challenges are and asking for help in these areas – and doing so without shame or apologies.

Since my diagnosis, I've become very intentional when deciding whose advice to take. There are a lot of people dispensing it, but only a few you should listen to. Many of the people giving ADHD advice, although well intentioned, don't seem to understand ADHD at all. They say things like 'just buy a planner' or 'just try to form a routine'. I can't tell you how many times I've screamed 'I've tried doing that!' at my phone screen while tripping over my pile of unused notebooks.

We need ADHD advice from people who actually understand ADHD, advice like the following:

- Invite a friend over or be in close proximity to someone and you will feed off their energy and find the motivation to start the task.

- Don't bother taking a screenshot on your phone because you'll forget to look at it. Write it down and put that bit of paper somewhere you walk past every day.

- There will be days when you won't be able to do anything except sit on the sofa and scroll social media and that's okay.

These are the tips we need, the real ones, the ones scattered throughout this book, the ones that actually come from someone who understands how our brains work.

Realizations

I've spoken to thousands of ADHDers since my diagnosis and one thing is glaringly obvious: millions of people are suddenly realizing that their personality 'flaws' were actually undiagnosed ADHD. And now every single thing in their past finally makes sense.

Why people said we were 'too much'.

Why our ex kept asking, 'What's wrong with you?'

Why all the easy jobs felt impossible.

Why, when we asked someone for traffic directions, we could never remember what they said.

Why we can hyper-focus but also why our excitement can wear down faster than others'.

Why we flared up in the face of rejection.

Why we felt like nothing about our personality was actually us.

We're not too much, there's nothing wrong with us. We just process things differently. And that's okay. The world is better when there is a diversity of minds because great minds think differently!

I am always saddened when I think about how many people, especially women and girls, grew up with no idea they were living with ADHD. They didn't have an explanation for why they operated differently from everyone else, no explanation for why they felt that they had to mask all the time.

> Women are three times less likely to receive an ADHD diagnosis.[1]
>
> Women are more likely to internalize their symptoms.
>
> Women are more likely to be overlooked.
>
> Women are feeling misunderstood.
>
> Women are being let down.

I've invited so many amazing women onto *ADHD Chatter*, which will elevate their voice and spread vital awareness. There is still a lot of work to do, but change is happening!

Embracing my differences

Like so many of us, my ADHD shows up in mysterious ways and I've fully embraced my differences. For example, I doodle in meetings. I'm not being rude. It helps me focus on what you're saying. My right foot will be shaking. I'm not bored. My excess energy has to go somewhere; otherwise, it will turn into anxiety. I might appear to zone out. I'm not daydreaming. I'm zoning in on my thoughts.

When I explain my ADHD to someone at work and they say, 'Everyone gets overwhelmed sometimes', I reply with this analogy: 'True, but everyone urinates, too, but if someone was doing it 40 times a day, I would say they had a problem.' Feel free to use it, too.

I got my ADHD diagnosis two years ago and it changed my life. Before my diagnosis, I didn't understand why I struggled so much. After my diagnosis, my life made sense. ADHD was the reason I was allergic to the boring stuff. But it's also the reason I'm:

- creative

- great in a crisis

- intuitive

- resilient

- hyper-focused

- spontaneous

- entrepreneurial

- empathetic

- a risk taker

- courageous.

And that's just the tip of the iceberg.

My ADHD shows up in so many amazing (and often contradictory) ways. Three ways my ADHD showed up this week:

- I bought three domains I will never use.

- I forgot to pay a parking fine, so it doubled.

- I've left the damp washing in the machine, again.

Three more ways my ADHD showed up this week:

- The *ADHD Chatter* podcast socials hit 800,000 followers.

- My DMs are overflowing with people showing their gratitude.

- I hyper-focused on writing this book.

ADHD has its challenges. The 'ADHD tax' is real. But it's also *enabling* me to do amazing things. I love my ADHD. I wouldn't swap it for anything.

I have always felt different. I've never had a good relationship with alcohol. I got kicked out of university. But when I stopped trying to 'fit in' and started to live my life in line with how my brain works, I:

- founded two global social media brands

- talked on stages all over the world

- trekked Mount Everest.

Before my ADHD diagnosis, I thought I:

- was unprofessional

- had to try really hard just to be 'normal'

- felt weird because I didn't work in the conventional 9–5 time slot.

After my ADHD diagnosis, I:

- judged myself on my output, not on how 'professional' I was

- accepted that the word 'normal' is meaningless

- felt empowered to work during the 'my brain is optimal' time slot.

My mind isn't suited to most conventional working processes. When I realized that, I thrived. Both professionally and personally. The moment I stopped trying to be 'normal' was the moment I started to shine.

Everyone has ADHD these days. It must be a new trend. Nothing makes me more furious than when I hear someone say this.

Look, let me explain, just because more people are being diagnosed with ADHD does not mean that everybody has ADHD. It might mean that our society is simply becoming much more self-aware. Instead of just gritting their teeth and getting on with it, countless people are suddenly realizing there's a reason why they're anxious, exhausted and overwhelmed all the time, and they're seeking answers.

So, no, everybody doesn't have ADHD these days, it's just that lots of us are playing catch-up and that should be applauded.

ADHD hacks that actually work

I thought I would use the last section to list all the ADHD hacks I have picked up along the way, the ones I wish I had known when I was younger, ones that actually work, not those that imply you simply need to work harder.

So, without further ado, in no particular order, here's a list of 'hacks' that have actually improved my life.

THE DOUBLE CHECK

Always double check your surroundings before you get off a train, get out of a taxi or leave a cafe. I can't tell you how many times I have left something behind, like keys or my phone, and how a simple double check would have saved me so much stress.

A simple glance back at your seat as you walk away is a game changer.

THE WALL OF POCKETS

Create (or buy) a collection of pockets and hang them
by the entrance of your home. Label each one with your
most commonly used items and leave lots blank for new
items. Think keys, passports, phones and meds. If you
wear glasses/contact lenses, always keep a spare pair in
one of the pockets.

PLAN YOUR DAY THE NIGHT BEFORE

My brain is best at night and it's terrible in the
morning. There's nothing worse than waking up, being
overwhelmed with all the tasks you need to do, being
unable to prioritize them and therefore doing nothing.

Use your best brain to help your struggling brain. It
really helps to wake up with a pre-written 'to do' list,
written the night before by your best brain. You can
thank your past self for helping you avoid task paralysis.

KEEP SHOPPING BAGS IN THE CAR

I'm terrible at remembering to pick up my reusable
shopping bags when I'm leaving my flat. It's so infuriating
when you get to the checkout, only to realize you've
forgotten your bags and have to buy a new one, again.

A game changer for me was when I saved the supermarket
car park location on my Google Maps, so whenever I drove
into the car park, my phone notified me to 'Grab a bag
from the back seat'.

BUY PRE-CHOPPED

I have lost track of times I've bought fresh vegetables, used some, forgotten about the rest, only to find them four weeks later, furry, at the back of the fridge.

Buying frozen pre-chopped vegetables put me back in charge of my life: fact.

KEEP A TOOTHBRUSH NEXT TO YOUR BED

It'll remind you to brush your teeth, trust me. Also, if you're lying in bed and you can't find the energy to move to the bathroom, cleaning with a dry brush is better than not cleaning them at all.

Gross? Maybe. Will it save you a costly trip to the dentist? Probably.

ORGANIZE THE FLOORDROBE

Fed up with picking up clothes from the floor and doing the sniff test to decide whether or not you can wear them again? Have baskets in your bedroom and label them 'Clean', 'Dirty' and 'Not dirty but not clean'. Game changer.

DON'T MAKE CLEANING HARDER

I used to store all my cleaning equipment in a cupboard in the kitchen. This is what neurotypicals do and it works well for them. Does it work for me? No! Let me explain.

Here's how I used to clean:

1 Go to the toilet.

2 Notice the bathroom needs cleaning.

3 Think, 'I need to get the cleaning equipment from the kitchen cupboard.'

4 Walk to the kitchen.

5 Get distracted by something in the kitchen.

6 Forget about the dirty bathroom.

I now keep a separate set of cleaning equipment in every bathroom, which enables me to keep on top of the cleaning as soon as I notice it needs doing. My bathrooms have never been cleaner!

DON'T EMPTY YOUR DISHWASHER

Your dishwasher is a secret extra cupboard nobody knows about. Seriously, just take the clean plates out when you need to use them.

UPSTAIRS/DOWNSTAIRS

For similar reasons as with the cleaning products, it's a good idea to have pairs of important items (vacuum cleaner, scissors, sticky tape, iron) and store one upstairs and one downstairs. It's an expense, but it makes them more accessible and it'll save you a lot of stress.

HOOKS INSTEAD OF HANGERS

I still don't understand why people use hangers when they can use hooks – so much easier.

You can have a dopamine-fuelled trip to the hobby shop to buy the hooks and turn the wardrobe modification into your most recent hyper-focus.

FINISH IT, THROW IT, BIN IT

How many times have you finished a bottle of shampoo, put it on the shower shelf or edge of the bath, got out, dried yourself and completely forgotten about throwing the empty shampoo bottle away?

Solution? Throw the shampoo bottle on the bathroom floor as soon as it's empty. You'll see it when you get out and you'll eventually pick it up and throw it away.

FIGHT THE URGE TO SIT DOWN IMMEDIATELY

When you get home from work, it's so tempting to throw yourself on the sofa and say, 'I'll put the rubbish out later. I'll make dinner later. I'll get changed out of my work clothes later.' It's a trap for us ADHDers.

Unless you're feeling particularly drained, I'd recommend maintaining your momentum: do as many small tasks as you can before you sit down on the sofa. Sitting down can instantly suck the energy out of us. We get distracted by our phones, we see something on Netflix, we find a

YouTube wormhole and suddenly three hours go by and we haven't eaten and we're still wearing our work clothes.

IF I DON'T WRITE SOMETHING DOWN, IT DOESN'T EXIST

Write everything down. Appointments, birthdays, ideas, thoughts, everything: write them down as they happen or they will be lost forever.

Use your visual calendar and set reminders. Have a pen and paper next to your bed. Hang whiteboards in every room of your house. Even next to the toilet because that's where the best ideas can happen! Get a waterproof one for the shower.

THE TASK BRACELET SYSTEM

Buy or create a bunch of bracelets and assign each one to a separate task – for example, making the bed, vacuuming the flat and doing the laundry. Start the day by wearing all the bracelets that are assigned to the tasks you need to complete that day. As you complete the task, take off the bracelet and place it in a bowl.

The bracelets do two things: they remind you that you need to do the task and they'll give you a big dopamine hit when you eventually take them off and place them in the bowl.

DON'T RELY ON YOUR BRAIN TO MONITOR TIME

Seriously, it took me 35 years to realize that five minutes is not as much time as I thought. Time and time again, I thought it was enough time to shower, get ready and leave the house, and time and time again, I was wrong.

Five minutes is only 300 seconds. As soon as I had that realization, I stopped thinking I had enough time to do multiple tasks.

Also, using timers has been a game changer for me. Something needs to go in the oven for 20 minutes? No problem. I can predict how long 20 minutes is. Wrong. I've lost track of how many times I've opened the oven to find a rock-solid bit of charcoal staring at me.

Use a timer for everything.

IGNORE THE 'COMMON SENSE' STUFF

A lot of productivity hacks that appear to be common sense actually don't work for me. For example, if I see something on my phone that I want to remember, common sense would say to take a screenshot. In reality, however, the screenshot will end up with the thousands of other screenshots on my phone and I'll forget to ever look at it.

Now, when I see something on my phone, I write it down immediately and keep it somewhere visual, such as on one of the whiteboards hanging in my flat, or if I'm out and about, I take a screenshot but then immediately make that screenshot the background image on my phone.

Another example of the 'common sense' stuff is the use of notebooks. I understand why people who don't understand ADHD would suggest 'just buy a notebook', but the reality is that I'll forget to use it, or if I do use it, I'll forget to keep using it, therefore rendering the whole process pointless.

The moment I started ignoring the 'common sense' stuff was the same moment I started to thrive.

RUN, FORREST, RUN!

We've heard it time and time again, but exercise really is the best thing for the ADHD mind.

I'm a big fan of running. It channels my hyperactivity into a subconscious movement, thereby allowing my mind to be free of the internal chatter that's normally there when I'm sitting down. It's why I'm a big advocate for companies to incorporate movement into meetings and work stations.

I have my best ideas when I'm moving. I have my worst ideas when I'm sitting still. Take it a step further by buying a standing desk. They're a bit expensive, but look at it as another example of paying the ADHD tax up front.

PROTEIN FOR LUNCH, CARBS FOR DINNER

My brain instantly becomes foggy after a heavy carb meal. I now intentionally avoid carbs at lunch. The impact on my focus and productivity has been immense.

THROW STUFF AWAY

It's not easy, but try not to hoard stuff that isn't a) sentimental or b) serving you in a positive way.

Clutter is a distraction for us ADHDers. It adds more chaos to an already chaotic mind. Keep bins in every room of your house and become an expert at throwing away unwanted stuff.

DELETE OR TAKE BREAKS FROM SOCIAL MEDIA

This one is really hard because the social media sites are literally designed to give us what we crave: dopamine. At least try to limit your usage and try not to look at your phone first thing in the morning. You wouldn't let 100 people into your bedroom, so try not to let them into your mind. Wake up, tick off a few tasks, get rid of a few of those bracelets I spoke about earlier, then reward yourself with some social media use.

The truth is, however, that you can have all the hacks in the world and still not feel secure and happy. As helpful as coping mechanisms can be, they also serve as a reminder of your differences.

We shouldn't need to 'hack' our way through life, we should be able to act as our true selves and function as we feel comes naturally. Of course, in reality, we are living in a neurotypical world, so, because of this, little hacks are useful, but we need to remind ourselves that they're not required because of a fault in us but because of a fault in the world that we live in: it hasn't caught up yet.

When we tell ourselves 'it's not our fault', we can strip away the layers of shame that have built up over years of being told we're broken. The ability to do this comes from a deep understanding of self and an awareness of the fact that you don't need to change who you are because who you are is enough.

That person who said you were 'too much', your ex who kept calling you 'lazy', the relative who called you 'rude' – they were all wrong.

We can all look back at our lives through a lens of grief and feel sad for the younger version of us who felt confused, but we can also look forward with a lens of understanding and kindness.

We are all amazingly unique, but we also share so many incredible qualities.

Thank you for coming on my journey with me and thank you for sharing yours with me.

It's my hope that in sharing stories with each other, we can all find our tribe, feel less alone, open up conversations and make the world a more accommodating place for all of us.

Endnotes

Chapter 1

1 'How Much of Communication Is Nonverbal?', The University of Texas Permian Basin. https://online.utpb.edu/about-us/articles/communication/how-much-of-communication-is-nonverbal/#:~:text=The%2055%2F38%2F7%20Formula&text=It%20was%20Albert%20Mehrabian%2C%20a,%2C%20and%207%25%20words%20only

Chapter 2

1 Maskell, L. (2022) *ADHD: An A–Z*. Jessica Kingsley Publishing.

2 Dodson, William. 'ADHD and the Epidemic of Shame', *ADDitude*, 22 August 2022. www.additudemag.com/slideshows/adhd-and-shame/

3 McDowall, Almuth, Doyle, Nancy, and Kiseleva, Meg. (2023) *Neurodiversity at Work 2023: Demand, Supply and a Gap Analysis*. University of London. www.berkshirehealthcare.nhs.uk/media/109514758/neurodiversity-in-business-birkbeck-university-of-london.pdf

Chapter 3

1 Rehabs.uk website: https://rehabsuk.com/addictions/
   drug/adhd-specialist-addiction-treatment/

Chapter 7

1 SEND Reform England. (2023) *The Journey into
   S.E.N.D. Motherhood: Finding the End of the Rainbow.*
   www.amazon.co.uk/Journey-Into-S-N-D-
   Motherhood-ebook/dp/B0CNTNVC1W

Chapter 10

1 Kinman, Tricia. 'Gender Differences in ADHD
   Symptoms', healthline, 22 March 2016. https://
   www.healthline.com/health/adhd/adhd-symptoms-
   in-girls-and-boys#ADHD-and-Gender-

Acknowledgements

This book would not have been possible without my partner, Tanya, who supported my chaotic writing style and who gave me feedback in a way that didn't flare my RSD. Tanya, your understanding of ADHD throughout the writing process helped me enormously.

Thank you to my family, Mum, Dad, James and Jessica for your constant encouragement.

I would like to thank Outreach Talent Group and, in particular, Niamh, for sensitively reminding me of the deadlines.

Thank you to my publisher, in particular Victoria, for sharing my vision and coordinating the whole process in a way that worked with my brain.

Index

24-hour rule to requests 54–5
acceptance in relationships 113–15
accommodations for ADHD 32–40, 155
accountability 55–7, 174–7
addictions 62–4, 66–8
ADHD: An A–Z (Maskell) 26
ADHD Chatter xi, 164–5, 173, 189,
    225, 227
ADHD Women's Wellbeing (podcast) 42
ADHD WISE 147
ADHD Works 26
advance planning 230
affection 106
alcohol 59–62, 64–6, 68–70, 86, 227
anxiety 49–52
apologizing 197–8
arguments 202–7
asking for positive feedback 31–2
automation in business 187–8

body doubling 57, 103–5, 152, 175
bonding with children 147–9
boredom avoidance 165
boundary setting 77–9
budgeting 133–5
burnout 42–4, 55, 139, 146, 164, 167,
    170–2
business
    accountability in 174–7
    automation in 187–8
    boredom avoidance 165
    burnout 164, 167, 170–2
    experiences of 159–61
    feedback in 183–4
    gamifying tasks 168–70
    Idea Shelf 162
    imposter syndrome 172–7, 186–7, 190
    improvising in 190–1
    identifying good business ideas 161–5
    pace of running 188–9
    routines in 167
    self-accommodations in 177–83

    self-awareness in 184–7
    skills learning 166–7
    stagnation prevention 165–70

celebrating wins 27
children with ADHD 153–7
cleaning equipment 231–2
clothes organizing 231
coaches for ADHD 26
Cognitive Behavioural Therapy (CBT)
    139–40
'common sense' stuff 235–6
communication in relationships 110–11,
    194, 196–7, 200, 206–7
community 66–8
covering up difference 1–4, 16–18

dating person with ADHD 211–14
decision paralysis 10–11, 75, 210, 219
diagnosis of ADHD 15–16
difference
    covering up 1–4, 16–18
    decision paralysis 10–11
    diagnosis of ADHD 15–16
    driving 11–12
    embracing 225–9
    eye contact 6–8
    friendships 12–15
    heightened intuition 8–10
    justice sensitivity flare-ups 4–6
    masking 16–18
    out of sight, out of mind 12–15
    unmasking 18–21
dishwasher emptying 232
Doherty, Karen 193, 194, 196, 198, 201
double-checking 229–30
driving 11–12
Drynan, Lottie 148, 150

Ehmen, Christian 17
embracing difference 225–9
embracing strengths 27–34

exercise 236
explaining ADHD to the boss 34–5
eye contact 6–8, 29

failing relationships 201–2
Fairbairns, Ruari 68–9
feedback in business 183–4
fun in relationships 209–10

gamifying tasks 57–8, 168–70
gender and ADHD 218, 224–5
good intentions 91–3
Grainger, Hester 154–6
Gupwell, Matt 64, 66, 68
friendships 12–15

hacks for ADHD
    advance planning 230
    cleaning equipment 231–2
    clothes organizing 231
    'common sense' stuff 235–6
    dishwasher emptying 232
    double-checking 229–30
    exercise 236
    hooks for clothes 233
    meal planning 2237
    momentum after work 233–4
    pre-chopped vegetables 231
    shopping bags in car 230
    social media breaks 237–8
    task bracelets 234
    teeth cleaning 231
    throwing things away 233, 237
    timers 235
    writing things down 2234
Hadley, Kirsti 144
Hallowell, Edward 63–4
heightened intuition 8–10
helping out 111–13
Hiew, Samantha 82–3, 84
Hill, Jodie 37, 38
hooks for clothes 233
hyper-focus 40–4

Idea Shelf 162
importance of ADHD 220–3
imposter syndrome 25, 172–7, 186–7, 190

improvising in business 190–1
impulse spending 117–35
impulsivity in relationships 106–7
info dumping 98, 99–103, 115, 122

journalling 26, 37, 54, 162, 165, 170,
    171–2, 173, 209
Journey into S.E.N.D. Motherhood, The
    (Hadley) 144
justice sensitivity flare-ups 4–6

knee-jerk reactions 29–31
Kostrewa, Geraldine 139–40

LADBible 33, 41, 53, 56, 59, 164, 166,
    168
letter-writing to self 27

Maskell, Leanne 26, 27
masking 16–18
Mathams, Tina 121, 122, 133, 134
McLaughlan, David 62, 63, 76
meal planning 237
misconceptions about ADHD 218–19
momentum after work 233–4
Moryoussef, Kate 42–3

Neurodiversity Networks CIC 147

out of sight, out of mind 12–15

pace of running businesses 188–9
parenting
    bonding with children 147–9
    children with ADHD 153–7
    experiences of 137–42
    perfectionism in 139–42
    preparing for 142–5
    and rejection 152–3
    reminders for 147
    shame in 150–2
    slot protection 145–7
parking fines 126–7
pausing responses 87–90
perfectionism 139–42
Perfectly Autistic 154
Perryman, Janine 147–8

positive feedback 31–2
positive traits of ADHD 24–6
pre-chopped vegetables 231

quality time 111

rejection
    and alcohol 86
    and biology 85–6
    boundary setting 77–9
    experiences of 71–3
    good intentions 91–3
    and parenting 152–3
    pausing responses 87–90
    rejection sensitive dysphoria 73–7,
        80–93, 152–3, 198–200, 203
    in relationships 84–5, 198–200
    saying 'let me think about it' 77–9
    saying 'no' 79–80
rejection sensitive dysphoria 73–7,
    80–93, 152–3, 198–200, 203
relationships
    acceptance in 113–15
    ADHD impacts on 95–9, 193–7
    apologizing 197–8
    arguments in 202–7
    body doubling 103–5
    communication in 110–11, 194,
        196–7, 200, 206–7
    dating person with ADHD
        211–14
    fun in 209–10
    helping out 111–13
    impulsivity in 106–7
    info dumping 99–103
    misunderstandings in 210–11
    quality time 111
    and rejection 84–5, 198–200
    self-worth in 207–9
    showing affection 106
    signs of failing 201–2
    triggers in 194–5, 201
    understanding ADHD in 107–10
    urgency in 105

reminders for parenting 147
routines in business 167

saying 'let me think about it' 77–9
saying 'no' 79–80
self-accommodations in business 177–83
self-awareness in business 184–7
self-worth in relationships 207–9
shame shame 19–20, 45, 49, 68, 70, 75,
    78–9, 87, 102, 107–9, 113–4, 120,
    122, 126–7, 130–1, 134–5, 139, 143,
    150–2, 207, 222–3, 238
shopping bags in car 230
social media breaks 237–8
slot protection 145–7
stagnation prevention 165–70
strengths of ADHD
    accommodations for ADHD 32–40
    asking for positive feedback 31–2
    celebrating wins 27
    coaches for 26
    embracing strengths 27–34
    explaining ADHD to the boss 34–5
    hyper-focus 40–4
    journalling 26, 37
    knee-jerk reactions 29–31
    leaning into 44–7
    letter-writing to self 27
    positive traits 24–6

task bracelets 234
teeth cleaning 231
Templeton, Sarah 150–1, 153–4
throwing things away 233, 237
timers 235
triggers 194–5, 201

UNILAD 41, 45–6, 52–3, 54, 56, 59–60,
    164–5
unmasking 18–21
urgency in relationships 105

Whittington, Eric 14–15
writing things down 53–4, 234